THE
MAKING OF AMERICA
SERIES

GAITHERSBURG

HISTORY OF A CITY

This 1980s photograph shows fishing at Summit Hall Pond.

THE
MAKING OF AMERICA
SERIES

GAITHERSBURG
HISTORY OF A CITY

CITY OF GAITHERSBURG

ARCADIA

Published by Arcadia Publishing,
an imprint of Tempus Publishing, Inc.
2 Cumberland Street
Charleston, SC 29401

Printed in Great Britain.

Library of Congress Catalog Card Number: 2002103801

For all general information contact Arcadia Publishing at:
Telephone 843-853-2070
Fax 843-853-0044
E-Mail sales@arcadiapublishing.com

For customer service and orders:
Toll-Free 1-888-313-2665

Visit us on the Internet at http://www.arcadiapublishing.com

CONTENTS

ACKNOWLEDGMENTS

The following people have contributed to the success of this book by supplying valuable information. A special thank you to Judith Christensen of the Gaithersburg Historical Association.

Mr. and Mrs. Howard S. Abel, Winnie Allen, Mary Anderson, Richard Arkin, Lois King Aschenbach, Merle Barbour, Joseph R. Beall, Lemuel Beall, Mr. and Mrs. E. Gorden Bell, Estelle Waters Bell, Ruth Belt, Genevieve Selby Benson, Frank Berfield, Richard Biggs, Richard Blohm, Juanita German Bohrer, Marjorie Briggs Bohrer, Lorrene Border, Sandra Bourdeaux, Helen D. Bowman, Ruth Perry Bowman, Barbara Braymer, Betty Meem Brewington, Raymond Briggs, Arthur P. Brigham, the Brookings Institute, William L. Broomall, Dr. Frank Broschart, Mary Brown, Elizabeth Stone Brunett, Maude Duvall Burks, Virginia C. Burruss, Gail Butler, Irene Byrne, Nora Caplan, Catherine Caponiti, Lula McBain Carlisle, Heather Carmen, Dr. Douglas Chandler, Jay Christensen, Judith Christensen, Mollie Christie, Nina Clarke, Chris Clifford, Valerie Cooke, Eileen Corbitt, Mac G. Corrin, Priscilla Cram, Hilda Cross, Suzanne Crowder, Ruby Briggs Crown, Eleanor W. Cunningham, The Reverend Harry Dalzell, Evelyn Darby, George Darby, Mrs. Lawrence Darby, Ruth Darby, Robert Davidson, Winfred E. Davis, Mrs. Walter Deppa, Carroll Martin Diamond, Virginia Dietz, Daniel Dowd, Dorothy Phebus Drew, Steve Duckworth, Alfred Duvall, Cuyler Duvall, Pearl M. Duvall, Woodrow W. Duvall, Mr. and Mrs. Elwood Easton, Mary Murphy Easton, Irene Schwartz Emmet, Ralph Etchison, Diane Evenline, Tim Faust, Mr. and Mrs. Sonny Feldman, William Fenton, A. Merle Ferguson, Mike Ferguson, Helen Fisher Fiala, Syd Fishman, Jennifer Fortin, Rita English Frank, Jimmy Frazier-Bey, Hebb Freeman, Alice Diamond French, Irving Fulks, Leona Fulks, McKendree G. Fulks, Agnes "Jackie" Gaither, The Gazette Newspapers, Glenn Gilliam, Mr. and Mrs. Carlton Gloyd, Mary E. Gloyd, Mr. and Mrs. Bruce Goldensohn, Frank Goldstein, Carrie Browning Green, Susan B. Green, Clarice Kingsley Griffith, Jane Clements Griffith, Lycurgus M. Griffith III, Nellie Briggs Groshon, Marshall Grotenhius, Ann Watkins Gue, Janet Gunn, Eric D. Halgele, Harry W. Hammann, Kathleen E. Hanna, James W. Hansen, Mr. and Mrs. B.Z. Harding, Charles M. Harris, Daniel Hassett, Ella E. Hawkins, Rona Hollander, Dorothy Horst, Grace Hudgins, Bonnie Hum, Carol Hunsecker, The Reverend James M. Hunt, Dave Hyatt, Betty Isis, Mr. and Mrs. Charles T. Jacobs, Mr. and Mrs. Merle T. Jacobs, Lucille B. Jarell,

Mary Jenkins, David Johnson, Pete Jones, The Journal Newspapers, Denny Katzen, Carroll Kearns, Walter Keir, Barbara Walker Kettler, Beatrice King, Mr. and Mrs. Donald King, Hilda Walker King, Mr. and Mrs. W. Lawson King, Nancy Kirk, Gwinn Kirkman, David Kirtin, Carol Klein, The Reverend Ronald Klein, Dorothy Krikorian, Dorothy Kurtz, Gus Lamparis, Olive Larcombe, The Reverend Ronald E. Libby, Gail Littlefield, Rebecca Miller Lipford, Mr. and Mrs. Harold Logan, Greg Lresik, Helena Madison, John W. Magruder, Mary Gorden Malloy, Pete Manus, Laverne Mason R.N., Lucy F. McBain, Mr. and Mrs. L. Clark McCutcheon, Janet McFadden, Eileen McGuckian, E. Dale Meadows, Harry C. Meem, Janet Etchison Miles, Patricia Duvall Miles, Pina Jo Miller, Maxine Coleman Mills, Mr. and Mrs. Sidney Mills, Catherine Gartner Mocarskyt, Juanita Moore, Rita Moroney, Mr. and Mrs. Harold C. Morris, Webster Moxley, Harry Mullican, Charles E. Nicholson, Susan E. Nicholson, George S. Northam, Michael Novak, The Reverend Herbert Nunley, Suzanne M. Offutt, Dr. I. David Oler, James Oliver, Claude Owen, Margaret Pearson, Richard Perry, Marie Pincus, Lloyd A. Phoebus, Charles N. Phoebus, Nettie Phoebus, Thomas W. Phoebus, Thomas Plummer, Katherine R. Poole, Pastor Donald Pope, The Reverend Ralph D. Posey, Edna Peddicord Price, Naomi Thompson Ray, Annie Reinhart, Jack Roach, Daniel C. Robertson, Elizabeth Robertson, Katherine Robertson, Carolyn Rodeffer, James Rowland, Maureen Ruppert, Mrs. Lester Saffell, John Sage, Rosabel Gartner Sandison, The Reverend Edwin Schell, Rosalie Shantz, Jane Davis Shaub, The Reverend Charles Shepherd, The Reverend B.W. Shoemaker, Rena Shifflet, Bette Shumaker, Ethel Sinn, Frances Fitzgerald Smith, Gail E. Smith, Lucy N. Smith, Mary Beth Smith, Ronald E. Smith, Sally Smith, Susan Smith, Mary Snouffer Spangler, George Spatafore, Maurice Spaulding, Rebekah English Speich, Lichter Stein, Richard Stewart, Armenia Briggs Stup, Father Basil Summer, Jeanette Sweadner, Jane C. Sween, Angela Swope, Helen Walker Talbott, The Reverend Anna L. Talley, David Tao, Gladys Fraley Thompson, Honora Thompson, Warren G. Thompson, Howard Trager, Paul Vanderstice, William C. VanDerWeele, Mrs. Carl VanDiver, Katharyne Severance Van Metre, Barbara Badger Vann, John Vaskoe, Kathryn Walder, Charles R. Walker, Constance Walker, Mr. and Mrs. Grover Walker, Mr. and Mrs. Milton Walker, Ralph Walker, George Wallrodt, Mark Walston, Daisy Bell Ward, George H. Ward, Mary B. Ward, Nettie Dorsey, Etchison Watkins, Marie Wayne, James T. Weaver Jr., The Reverend and Mrs. Herman M. Wilson, Robert Wilson D.D.S., Roscoe N. Whipp, Barbara Harding White, W. Rodney White Jr., Bill Wilmot, Koko Wittenburg, May Wong R.N., Sara Beall Wooden, Anna J.L. Young, Jim Young, Paul Young, and Barbara Zanner.

INTRODUCTION

The community that became Gaithersburg first appeared in the mid-1750s when several Maryland landowners established plantations northwest of the future site of Washington, D.C. A few families formed a community known as Logtown at Summit Hall, and to the west was Zoar, a 1,238-acre plantation owned by Gerard Briscoe and his family. South of Logtown was Mudtown and the Clements family farms, with Deer Park situated between the Clements land and Logtown.

To the north of Logtown, Henry B. Brookes amassed a large plantation of more than 1,000 acres. His son-in-law Benjamin Gaither settled on his wife's dower property near the intersection of present-day Diamond and Frederick Avenues before 1800 and started a blacksmith shop, store, and tavern to serve travelers and locals. His crossroads enterprise became known as Gaithersburg.

When U.S. postal service began in 1851 the post office was located in the Gaither store, by then renamed the Forest Oak Store, which stood near the famous "Forest Oak" tree. This mailing address of Forest Oak was subsequently adopted by some as the village's name in the nineteenth century.

But Gaithersburg became the official name when the village legally incorporated on April 5, 1878. The name honored the founding family but was also perhaps meant to recognize General William Lingan Gaither, who influenced the Baltimore & Ohio Railroad (B&O) to build its line through the town in 1873.

The Forest Oak tree near Gaither's old store witnessed much change along the "great road west," which has been known at times as Maryland Route 240 and 355 and also as Frederick Avenue, in its nearly 300 years of life. The tree saw famous men such as George Washington and Edward Braddock traveling between Georgetown and Frederick, Union and Confederate forces during the Civil War, and many settlers moving west. It watched transportation change from stagecoaches three times a week to high-speed automobile traffic, and it saw the crossroads store and tavern grow into the commercial development of the modern era. But in the summer of 1997, this natural landmark, which had become the city's official logo, was unfortunately uprooted in a storm.

The B&O Railroad spurred construction of hotels and rooming houses to serve the summer visitors leaving Washington, D.C. during the hot summer months. It also helped Gaithersburg's agricultural businesses flourish as area farmers were able to quickly ship produce and milk, and local stores could carry a broader range of inventory. Agriculture

This map shows Gaithersburg as it appeared in 1879.

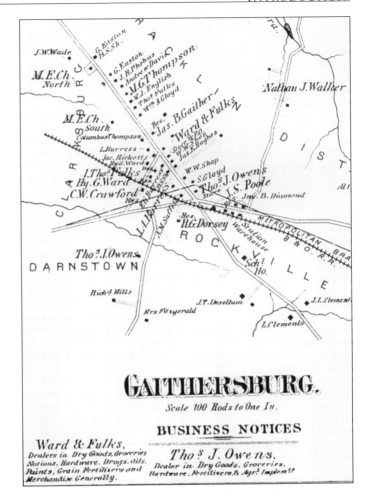

expanded and the town grew rapidly. Gaithersburg became known as "The Heart of Montgomery County" and adopted a sheaf of wheat as its official seal.

A residential and industrial boom followed the coming of the railroad. One of the new buildings was the present-day Gaithersburg City Hall, built in 1895. Earlier it was the site of the "World Famous Schwarz Peony Gardens," which boasted 410 varieties of peonies from all over the world. Each spring the garden became a tourist attraction visited by admirers, including President Woodrow Wilson. The city purchased the estate in 1958 and renovated it for use as municipal offices.

Gaithersburg's scientific contributions began in 1899 when the Gaithersburg Latitude Observatory was built as part of an international project to measure the Earth's wobble on its axis. The observatory and five others in Japan, Italy, Russia, and the United States gathered information that is still used by scientists today to determine polar motion and the physical properties of the Earth. Gaithersburg data is also used as a navigational aid for satellites. The station was in operation until 1982 when computerization rendered manual observation obsolete.

On June 14, 1961, the National Bureau of Standards (now the National Institute of Standards and Technology) broke ground on its first Gaithersburg building. The relocation of this government agency brought an incredible amount of growth to the city and started today's research and development industry. The influx of scientific research that followed inspired Gaithersburg to discard its old sheaf-of-wheat seal and adopt a new one, which features an office building and the motto "Science Capital of the United States," when it legally changed to city status in 1968.

Gaithersburg has seen significant change in recent years. The old crossroads village is now a bustling suburb of Washington, D.C. It has become a regional center for high-technology companies and a biotechnology hub, while commercial agriculture is close to non-existent. The rolling fields of wheat are now roads, housing developments, and commercial enterprises, but at the same time a number of historic communities and traditions have been preserved. As the city thrives in the new millennium and continues to grow, it also aims to retain the best qualities of a small town with a rich, diverse heritage.

The grand Forest Oak tree witnessed Gaithersburg's growth through the years.

1. EARLY SETTLEMENT

The region of North America now known as Maryland was once the grounds of the Piscataway nation from the fall line of the Potomac River in Rockville to the Atlantic, and the realm of the Susquehannock nation west and north of the fall line, an area that included present-day Montgomery County.

Settlers moving up the Potomac River valley from Chesapeake Bay colonized the piedmont area of Montgomery County up to Great Falls. Gaithersburg, however, was not a water settlement. It had roads and trails instead of a river. The roads were established earlier by the Susquehannock or "Seneca" nation and provided a way into the interior of the land, away from the rivers. Frederick Avenue was first mapped as a Native American trail and then as the George Towne–Frederick Towne Road. In Gaithersburg the road is called Frederick Avenue and has always been the city's main street.

Gaithersburg was considered the last outpost of civilization in Montgomery County in 1730, but by 1750 most of the large tracts of land had been taken and only smaller unclaimed pieces were left. There were many large holdings in and around Gaithersburg before 1800. The names of Lost Knife, Shady Grove, Deer Park, and Quince Orchard have survived.

As the region was colonized by Europeans with horses and oxen, the road was widened and assigned to road supervisors. These were usually adjacent landowners directed to maintain passage and compensated by the county to fill ruts and low places with logs, stone, and dirt. As wagons, horses, oxen, and people needed occasional repairs and respite, services such as public houses, blacksmiths, and other trades also appeared along the road.

Gaithersburg was at the top of a steep outcropping defined by Seneca Creek on the north and Muddy Branch Creek on the south. With its shady groves of giant oak trees and good water, it was an ideal location for travelers to stop and rest, or even settle.

On Thursday, June 30, 1791, at a little after 4:00 in the morning, George Washington started from Georgetown toward Philadelphia. Being "desirous of seeing the Country North of Georgetown," he decided to travel the upper road that passed through Fredericktown in Maryland and through York and Lancaster in Pennsylvania, according to John C. Fitzpatrick's *The Diary of George Washington, 1748–1799*. Washington breakfasted at a small village he called Williamsburg (Rockville), passed by the courthouse of Montgomery County, dined at Peter's Tavern about 20 miles farther on, and arrived at Fredericktown around sunset. Washington described the road as rather hilly, the lands good and well timbered, and the farmhouses of a better kind than he expected to find.

Summit Hall is reminiscent of Gaithersburg's agricultural days. Frances Kellerman and friend stroll by the walnut trees in this 1937 photograph.

The small grain planted in the fields was thin, due to the extreme spring drought and to the frosts and lack of snow to cover the fields during the preceding winter. On this journey, Washington would have passed by a plantation and tavern located on what is now the King farm, as well as Robert Magruder's gate on property known as Mt. Pleasant where the Casey Barns are now located, several small log dwellings in the vicinity of the intersection of Muddy Branch and Route 355, the village of Logtown at Summit Hall Farm, Edward Burgess's store-house near Summit Avenue, and Henry Brookes's elegant plantation house known as Montpelier near present-day Montgomery Village Avenue.

AGRICULTURE AND TOBACCO

From 1700 to 1950, agriculture was the main industry in and around Gaithersburg. Most plantations raised food for their own consumption and for feed for their animals, which was called subsistence farming. The first money crop harvested in the region was tobacco, the production of which was very tedious and time consuming. Because of the large investment of time involved, tobacco was called an "18-month crop."

Tobacco from this part of Maryland was low-quality burley tobacco suitable for cigars, but not cigarettes. Linthicum and Hall operated two cigar factories in Gaithersburg until the late 1890s. In earlier days, however, London merchants wanted cigarette tobacco, so most of Montgomery County's tobacco was shipped to Scottish and Whitehaven merchants at Dumfried, Glasgow, and Cumberland.

During the depression of 1784 to 1815 neither corn, wheat, nor tobacco could pay the taxes. Many farms were sold for taxes at this time, but many others were just abandoned. By the end of the eighteenth century about two-thirds of the land in Montgomery County had been cleared, but years of tobacco growing had depleted the soil and many farmers shifted to wheat.

Isaac Weld, who traveled the road between Frederick and Georgetown in 1795, found the poverty of northern Montgomery County a striking contrast to the prosperity of the Frederick valley. About this time, a new form of agriculture came from the north with the Pennsylvania Germans and Quakers, whose farms of small grains, orchards, and cattle were dominated by large barns and fieldstone dwelling houses.

By the early 1800s local farmers had settled into a corn and wheat rotation and had added clover and pasture to the crop cycle. Future development depended upon the construction of canals, railroads, and highways to link the farmlands with the markets. A farm on a good road easily accessible from Georgetown, Washington, or Baltimore was worth more than a farm less favorably located.

After wheat or grain was harvested it had to be processed into an edible form, and the necessity of gristmills was recognized in colonial times. Most planters and farmers hauled their grain to a neighborhood mill and sent surplus bushels of wheat to Washington or Baltimore.

A good miller could make a small fortune. Today, we can still find ruins of these mills on the Seneca and Potomac Rivers and their tributaries. Clapper's Mill on Great Seneca Creek, Watkins, Walker's, Paw's, Davis's, and Goshen Mills were all located in the Gaithersburg farming area.

Businesses and plantations sprang up along the Georgetown to Fredericktown Road throughout the nineteenth century. The road furnished a means to take the local cash crop to the docks at Georgetown and to bring supplies back. A mail stagecoach began service in 1802, and by 1833, a daily stagecoach that brought passengers, mail, and goods left Georgetown at 3:00 a.m. and arrived at Campbell's tavern in Rockville for breakfast at about 9:00 a.m.

Many of the larger tracts and plantations at this time were the speculative investments of rich men far removed from Montgomery County. In Gaithersburg the landowner often lived on the property, though the actual farm labor was left to others. Tenant farmers often purchased their farms and sometimes the erstwhile tenant and gentry families intermarried, creating dynasties that survive today.

Later in the nineteenth century Gaithersburg became known as an agricultural service town on the railroad in the geographic center of Montgomery County, which led to its being known as "The Heart of Montgomery County." In the mid-twentieth century the Montgomery County Agricultural Board constructed new fair grounds in Gaithersburg on the old Meem farm convenient to the railroad stop on Chestnut Street.

The land along Frederick Avenue within the present-day Gaithersburg city limits remained largely intact and in agricultural use from 1700 to 1900. The southern portion on both sides of Frederick Avenue from Deer Park Road to Shady Grove Road was owned by the Magruder and Clements families with the exception of Oakmont, a residential subdivision allied to the Washington Grove Campground Association. Several large landowner families—the Brookes, Gaither, and Thompson families—owned the north end of town from Diamond Avenue beyond Montgomery Village Avenue. Very little subdivision was done on this property before 1900. The early commercial and residential development in Gaithersburg was located between present-day Odend'Hal and Summit Avenues along Frederick Avenue.

Today agriculture does not have the influence in Montgomery County that it once had, and in the Gaithersburg area it is close to non-existent. The area is now a suburban city that has left its ties to agriculture in the past.

This early photograph shows harvesting at Summit Hall.

2. EARLY FAMILIES

Most early Gaithersburg settlers and landowners were related. The Burgess, Gaither, and Brookes families were related by blood and marriage as well as by landed interests. They were also in the same social class. Many eighteenth- and nineteenth-century marriages were celebrated as much for consolidating land and keeping it in the family as for producing heirs. This can be seen in the later marital history of these three families and in that of Benjamin Gaither's son James B. Gaither, whose grandfather was Henry Brookes.

THE BURGESS FAMILY

The first William Burgess in America was born *c*. 1622 in England. Records indicate that he was closely related to the Burgess family of Marlborough in Wiltshire. He was transported to Virginia prior to 1646, and in 1650, he moved to Anne Arundel County, Maryland. His first of three wives was Elizabeth Robbins by whom he had two children.

The Gaithersburg Burgess line descends from their first child, Edward Burgess II, born about 1655. He married Sarah Chew in All Hallow's (Episcopal) Parish in Anne Arundel County, and the couple had nine children. Their sixth, Sarah Burgess, was born about 1691 and married Benjamin Gaither on September 8, 1709.

This was not the Benjamin Gaither of latter-day Gaithersburg but his grandfather. The Edward Burgess who served in many governmental roles in Montgomery County and in the state of Maryland and who owned a store in Gaithersburg for a time was the younger Benjamin Gaither's cousin. Colonel Edward Burgess had extensive holdings in the vicinity of Summit Hall including a store on the Frederick Road at Logtown. He was the most prominent of the pre-1800 Summit Hall owners.

Through these connections Edward Burgess and his wife inherited "Benjamin's Lot," the original Gaither plantation. Burgess acquired a portion of "Snowden's Second Addition to his Manor," at 555 acres; "Silent Valley" and "Barnes Good Luck" upon the middle Bennett Creek; and "Resurvey on Younger Brother." The 1790 census reported Burgess as the head of a family with 19 slaves, but he suffered financial reversals and had to sell part of his assets before his death on December 5, 1809.

Edward Burgess moved to the Gaithersburg-Logtown area in 1773–1774, establishing his store and residence west of the Frederick Road on the ridge between the present Summit and DeSellum Avenues. When, in 1776, the Continental Congress resolved to establish a "Flying Camp" in the middle colonies, Burgess was among the first to answer the call to arms. Thereafter he led an active life in the affairs of the county, serving as a justice of the peace, a judge of the county court and levy court, a magistrate, and a member of the House of Delegates from 1777 to 1795. Burgess's sons did not leave any male heirs in Gaithersburg to continue the family name although his daughter Margaret married Ninian Clagget and his other daughter Mary married John Skekell.

THE GAITHER FAMILY

The Gaither family in America had its origin in the Jamestown Colony of Virginia and is one of the oldest families from the English colonies. The line can be traced back to 1620, when John Gater arrived and established himself among the James River settlements. After the great Native American massacre of 1622, the governor of Virginia ordered a census, or muster, of all subjects who survived the ordeal. On February 16, 1623, John Gater was listed among those living "at James Cittye and with the Coropracon thereof." At the next census, the "Muster of the Inhabitants att Mulbury Iland," taken on January 25, 1624, contained "John Gatter came in the George 1620."

John Gaither and his wife, Joan, of Elizabeth City, received 300 acres of land on the Eastern Branch of the Elizabeth River. They had a son, also named John. Tradition has it that John Gaither II was a dissenter, or Catholic, who accepted the invitation of Lord Baltimore to settle in Maryland where religious tolerance was granted to all Christians. He moved his wife, Mary, and son John III to Maryland and settled on the Severn River near Annapolis, but died shortly thereafter. On November 20, 1652, Thomas Hatton, the secretary of the province, granted the widow Mary Geather letters of administration as "widow and relict of John Geather late of the County of Annarundel . . . deceased."

John Gaither III sold his land, and on January 26, 1663, he and Robert Proctor jointly patented "Abington," 875 acres between the North Run and South Run of the South River. Abington became the home of the family in Maryland.

John Gaither III married around 1676. He and his wife, Ruth, had seven children. Gaither fought in the Nanticoke Indian War of 1678 under Colonel William Burgess, and in 1681, he signed a document that declared him to be a captain of the royal government of the province. On February 9, 1685, Captain John Gaither III bought 150 acres of "Freemanston" from Edward Burgess, with Sarah Burgess relinquishing her third interest as his wife. When Captain Gaither died in 1702, the family estate Abington was left to his first son, John Gaither IV. His third son, Benjamin Gaither, received 252 acres in the fork of the Pautuxent River.

On September 8, 1709, Benjamin married Sarah Burgess, daughter of Edward Burgess and Sarah Chew Burgess. Benjamin and Sarah purchased another 200 acres in 1719 from Richard Snowden that became known as "Gaither's Fancy." They had 13 children. Their eighth child was Henry Gaither, born May 24, 1724, and was the father of the younger Benjamin Gaither.

Henry Gaither married Martha Ridgley, the daughter of William and Elizabeth Ridgley. He was appointed with others to raise $1,333 for arms and ammunition in the Revolutionary War for Montgomery County. In March 1778, he subscribed to the Oath

William Lingan Gaither influenced the B&O to build its line through Gaithersburg.

of Allegiance and Fidelity to the State of Maryland in Montgomery County before Magistrate Edward Burgess. He and Martha also had 13 children.

When the elder Benjamin Gaither died in 1741, he left his land and property to his children, with his wife, Sarah, retaining a life estate on the family plantation. Benjamin Gaither's personal property was appraised at more than 1,000 pounds sterling and included 14 slaves. Henry Gaither was left 350 acres known as "Gaither's Chance." The will was contested and not settled until 1788, but Henry had died in 1783 leaving his minor son Benjamin a 100-acre portion of "Moab" in Frederick County and 61 acres of "Presley." The elder Benjamin's brother Henry Chew Gaither was appointed guardian of Henry's minor children Benjamin and Daniel.

Benjamin Gaither of Gaithersburg, son of Henry and Martha Ridgley Gaither, was born about 1764 and died in 1838. He married Margaret Brookes, daughter of Henry C. and Martha (Bowie) Brookes of Montgomery County. In 1797, he deeded his legacy property "The Resurvey on Moab" to Ephraim Cane of Frederick. Margaret Gaither waived her dower interest. The couple took up residence on Margaret's dower property, 229 acres of Deer Park on Frederick Avenue.

THE BROOKES FAMILY

Henry Brookes ultimately owned more than 1,000 acres in and around Gaithersburg. His home "Montpelier," with 786 acres, was left in life estate to his wife, Martha, to convey to his son James Bowie Brookes on her death. One of the property lines of this tract went "to Benjamin Gaither's fence." Excepted from the transfer was the 1-acre family burying ground. This is presumably the Brookes family burying ground since it was excepted to Martha and James B. Brookes and would have been located at Montpelier, which was on the northwest corner of the intersection of Frederick and Montgomery Village Avenues. It is now commonly known as the "IBM site."

Henry Brookes left to his daughter Margaret Brookes Gaither and her daughters Martha and Eveline Gaither his interests in Deer Park, Montpelier, Younger Brother, and other tracts called Roses Delight and Point Lookout, as well as the whole of "Resurvey on Mill Tract." In 1838, Elijah Thompson made Montpelier his home and amassed about 700 acres stretching south down the west side of North Frederick Avenue. Thompson, who was born *c.* 1798, married Elizabeth Ricketts in 1825 and they had 13 children. His estate was partitioned among his heirs after his death in 1867.

The site of Henry Brookes's home became known as the "IBM site" in later years.

Montpelier is gone now, but Roger Brookes Farquhar wrote this description of the building in 1951:

> The house was of a pattern and size, which an aristocrat of southern Maryland would build as a manor house. It is fifty feet square and has a front hall eight feet wide from front to rear. The ceiling on the first floor is eleven feet high, foundation walls of brick are twenty-four inches thick, and the interior brick partitions are twelve inches thick. There are fireplaces and fine wooden mantels with hand carvings in the rooms. There are five fireplaces on the first floor and three on the second. On the right-hand side of the front hall is a handsome dining room with fireplace, behind which is a modern kitchen with a huge fireplace and crane. This room was the original detached kitchen with breezeway, but a second story with two rooms has been added.
>
> On the second floor there are three bedrooms on each side of the wide hall and two modern baths are now installed. Heavy oak beams, hewed on top, are visible in the cellar with the bark still in place on many of them. The outside of the main house has been covered with pebbledash (stucco) in recent times. The frame construction of the part of the rear of the side porch, including the bay window, is a recent addition.

"MR. GAITHERSBURG" AND THE KING FAMILY

Irvington Farm, William Lawson King's extensive dairy and cattle farm at the southwest corner of Frederick Avenue and Shady Grove Road, is today part of Rockville. But before the intervening farmland was divided into potential expansion area for adjacent municipalities, Irvington Farm and the King family were allied in agriculture, business, and family with Gaithersburg.

W. Lawson King acquired the first 122-acre parcel in 1925 from James W. Graff. Next, King bought the Frank Ricketts farm on Shady Grove Road, about 100 acres of cleared land that extended to the west side of present-day Interstate 270. He then purchased the Watkins Farm and the Fields Farm in 1940 and 1942 for his dairy operation. One was used for grazing land and the other for grain crops. Eventually King milked 100 cows every day and Irvington Farm was the largest single shipper of milk to Washington, D.C.

King was born and raised on a family dairy farm in Cedar Grove, Maryland. He married Cordelia Elizabeth Fulks in 1920. Cordelia's father, Thomas Iraneaus Fulks, was a businessman and farmer who lived at Newport Farm between Gaithersburg and Washington Grove and operated the hardware store in Gaithersburg that is now the Gaithersburg Rental Center. Cordelia was trained at a teacher's college in Washington, D.C. and taught at one-room schools in Dickerson and Quince Orchard, among others. She and King had three children: William Irving, known as "Billy;" Elizabeth Jeanne King; and Fannie Lois King.

W. Lawson King was already well schooled in dairy farming by his family when he bought the Graff Farm. The farm was named "Irvington" by Cordelia Fulks King after her brother Irving Fulks. For the first 14 years, all milking was done by hand and it took about two hours to milk 40 cows. The farm did not get milking machines until after 1939. Other than cows, the farm raised hay, corn, and grain to feed the livestock.

King was one of the first farmers to approach the dairy industry as a business. He was a businessman at heart and was enormously successful in his endeavors. In addition to farms from Cedar Grove to Darnestown, he owned and operated King Motor Company, which he opened in 1928 in the J.A. Belt Building in Gaithersburg. It later became King Pontiac and moved to a new showroom at 312 East Diamond Avenue in the 1950s. King expanded his automobile dealerships to Rockville and eventually consolidated them on a portion of Irvington Farm into King Pontiac-GMC.

King also owned a number of retail establishments in "Olde Towne" Gaithersburg, including most of the block containing Diamond Drug and the parking lot behind these buildings as well as other farms in Montgomery County. King was called "Mr. Gaithersburg" both for his business and his personal interest in the town's welfare.

Lois King Aschenbach relates that her father employed German POWs from the camp outside Gaithersburg on Snouffer School Road as farm hands. Because he was forbidden to pay them money, King gave them cigarettes every week. Lois said that she and a girlfriend got into the cigarettes and smoked them behind the barn. When her father figured out what they had done, instead of scolding them, he asked her if she would like to try a cigar. That, Lois said, cured her.

The former Mudtown property was associated with the W. Lawson King family through the next generation. King purchased property between Summit Hall and Irvington Farm, where the Muddy Branch crosses Frederick Avenue, as gifts for his daughters.

King Pontiac was located at 312 East Diamond Avenue in the 1960s.

Elizabeth "Betty" Jeanne King acquired 1.767 acres of the Offutt land by deed from Walter and Agnes G. Offutt in 1947. Betty Jeanne Jacobs said that her father, W. Lawson King, told her she had a choice of a lot or a car as a college graduation present. At the time she was engaged to be married and she chose a lot. When she acquired the lot it was a cornfield. The builder of the house at 1 Central Avenue was Harold Ward, a noted Gaithersburg builder, and as the design was similar to a house that Mrs. Jacobs had admired, she worked with the builder from some plans he already had.

On September 13, 1947, Betty Jeanne King married James Wriley Jacobs. His father was the superintendent of the Thomas and Sons Cannery on Chestnut Street so Dr. Jacobs's started his business career at a young age in the cannery. Dr. Jacobs was an educator in the Montgomery County public school system, but the Jacobs also had a local family business, Gaithersburg Farmer's Supply, which was located at the Washington Grove Granary on Railroad Avenue and Diamond Avenue/Route 124. After the Gaithersburg area became more urban, Gaithersburg Farmer's Supply went out of business and the Jacobs' three children and their families continued the business as Gaithersburg Ford/Kubota Tractor Company in a new facility across the street at 700 East Diamond Avenue.

The Kings continued the gift-lot tradition with their youngest child, Fannie Lois King. Lois married Conrad Victor Aschenbach in 1952. Conrad and Lois had four children and eventually took over the management of King Pontiac and other King automotive enterprises. In 1956, Walter C. Offutt sold 4.13 acres of land to William Lawson King. W. Lawson and wife Cordelia deeded 2.67 acres to Fannie Lois Aschenbach in 1959. This part of the parcel included the house at 539 South Frederick Avenue, which has become an unofficial landmark when entering Gaithersburg from the south.

THE FULKS FAMILY

The Fulks have been part of Gaithersburg's history since the 1760s. They did not start with land and position, but eventually achieved prominence in the community. Baltus Fulks was born before 1735 and died about 1806. He and his wife, Sarah, had five children. All but one married into local families: the Rawlings, Swamley, and DeSellum families. Exactly when Baltus Fulks arrived is not known, but his son was baptized in Prince George's Parish of the Episcopal Church in 1763. The first documented instance of the family is in 1773 when Gerard Briscoe of Frederick County, Virginia made over to Baltus Fulks "shoe maker" all his interest in two lots of land (1 acre) in Germansburg, or Logtown, where "said Baltus Fulks now lives." These two lots, parts of Deer Park and Roberts Delight, were deeded in 1806 by the heirs of Baltus Fulks to his daughter Catherine Fulks DeSellum and her husband, James DeSellum. Today they are part of Summit Hall Farm and Bohrer Park.

The Fulks' first child, William, was born in 1763. In 1789, Gerard Briscoe transferred 2.5 acres of land in Germansburg to William Fulks. The deed mentions that William Fulks had lived on the land since 1787. His occupation is not known, but in 1794, William transferred his land to Valentine Lingenfelder and moved to a farm near Hunting Hill. He sold this property in parcels, the last to the Clagett family in 1815. His son James died on October 31, 1816, and the family moved to Virginia.

After William Fulks's death, his son Ignatius returned to the Gaithersburg area. Ignatius Fulks was born on August 23, 1800 and died February 13, 1881. He married Henrietta Sanders, daughter of Captain James and Elizabeth Sanders of Anne Arundel County. By 1840, he was engaged in farming near the Muddy Branch Road. The Ignatius Fulks family had four children.

Their first son, James S., was listed in the 1850 census as a teacher. He then pursued a career in medicine, graduating from medical school in 1863. He also was appointed postmaster of the Forest Oak Post Office in 1863, position he held until 1866. He later practiced medicine in Baltimore, where he died in 1898.

Ignatius and Henrietta's second son, William Robert Fulks, was born in 1830 and married Mary Verlinda Ward in 1848. He was also a teacher and taught in both Frederick and Montgomery County, including the one-room school near Summit Avenue in Gaithersburg. He later operated two farms near Hunting Hill. He was a charter member of the Gaithersburg Grange and served as its first chaplain.

A third son, Ignatius Thomas Fulks, was born on July 7, 1832 and married Elizabeth Matilda Gloyd in 1869. She was the daughter of Samuel and Rebecca Ann (Swamley) Gloyd of Logtown. The couple had seven children.

Ignatius Thomas Fulks attended the Rockville Academy and taught school in Montgomery County for about 10 years. After this he became a member of the firm of Ward and Fulks, merchants, and continued in this business for 27 years. He was a major stockholder and president of the Gaithersburg Milling and Manufacturing Company. He was also a founder of the First National Bank of Gaithersburg and served on its board of directors, as well as being an officer of the Gaithersburg Mutual and Baltimore Building and Loan Associations, and a member of the Waverly Club. Fulks was instrumental in the incorporation of the town of Gaithersburg and was a member of the Gaithersburg Board of Commissioners from 1881 to 1884. He lived on Chestnut Street in 1878, but purchased Summit Hall Farm from his cousin John T. DeSellum in 1886 and made his home there.

Most of the children of Elizabeth and Ignatius T. Fulks remained in Gaithersburg. Thomas Iraneus Fulks was born in 1870 and married Frances Lois Williams in 1897. They built a new home on family land at 108 South Frederick Avenue, which is now a Gaithersburg historic site. T.I. Fulks was a businessman and farmer. He worked as a bookkeeper for the Gaithersburg Milling and Manufacturing Company and then opened a hardware store at 219 East Diamond Avenue. The old store is enclosed in the present brick building. Later, the T.I. Fulks family purchased a farm between Gaithersburg and Washington Grove that is now the site of Newport Estates, the Gaithersburg Middle School, and Villa Ridge. They also had a concrete block factory and a mill on their property, which was bisected by Route 124 and the B&O Railroad tracks. T.I. Fulks was a member of the town council from 1898 to 1906 and a founder of the first Gaithersburg Volunteer Fire Department in 1892. He was also a member of the Waverly Club and the Masonic Lodge.

The T.I Fulks' daughter Cordelia Elizabeth married William Lawson King in 1920, and their daughter Ruth married Millson Brandenburg. The T.I. Fulks' son Thomas Irving Fulks served on the Gaithersburg Town Council and was mayor from 1966 to 1978. He married Ida Kephart in 1927 and built the house now at 208 South Frederick Avenue.

This photograph of the Fulks house at 208 South Frederick Avenue was taken c. 1897.

Their children were Thomas Irving Jr. and Ruth Diane. Another son of I.T. Fulks, Edgar Fulks married Gertrude Elizabeth Walker. Their first daughter, Iva, married William T. Lewis, one of the developers of Observatory Heights. Another daughter Rosa Blanche married Frank Severance who was an officer of the First National Bank of Gaithersburg. They purchased a house that is now 205 South Summit Avenue and is owned by Ascension Episcopal Church. Oscar married Edith Watkins and worked in the family businesses.

THE GLOYD FAMILY

Samuel Gloyd, the son of Daniel and Joanna Gloyd, was born in 1763 in Prince George's County and died in 1846. Around 1790 he married Jane Sibley, and they had eight children. Their fourth child was Samuel Gloyd Jr., who was born in 1800.

The exact date of Samuel Gloyd Sr.'s arrival in Montgomery County is not known. A Jane Gloyd was issued a tavern license in 1820 and also was recorded as head of a household of five in the 1820 census, but Samuel Gloyd was not listed. The will of Samuel Gloyd was probated in 1846 and did not name any of his children except Eden, who was appointed executor. In 1847, his children Samuel, Eden, Elizabeth, Harriet, and Jane and a granddaughter Mrs. John Lowe, filed suit contesting the will. The assets listed in the case were household goods, two cows, and nine slaves. No business or land was noted.

Samuel Sylvester Gloyd (1841–1932) poses with his family. (Courtesy of Gary Gloyd.)

Samuel Gloyd Jr. was born October 24, 1800 and died in 1878. He married Rebecca Ann Swamley in 1827. They had 12 children who formed alliances with the Clements and other county families and dedicated their lives to the Catholic Church.

The first land record in Montgomery County for Samuel Gloyd Jr. is his purchase in 1841 of 5 acres, which consisted of part of "Valentine's Garden Enlarged" and part of "Two Brothers." This land was part of the estate of John Connell and had previously belonged to the Crabb family. It was located on the Frederick Road, but its proximity to Gaithersburg could not be determined. In 1844, Gloyd purchased 54.75 acres of land from Martha Gaither and Eveline (Gaither) Hughes. This was the property that is most often associated with the Gloyd family and is also the site of the famous Forest Oak.

As early as 1827 Samuel Gloyd Jr. is known to have operated a tavern in Montgomery County. The exact site is unknown and it is possible that it had more than one location. In 1833, a tax sale was held at the tavern of Samuel Gloyd Jr. The property being sold was located near Middlebrook, and since it was the custom of the day to hold these auctions near such property, it is likely that the tavern also was near Middlebrook at one time. Although the last entry in the tavern ledger is dated 1875, it does not appear in the licenses issued in Montgomery County for the years 1852 to 1863. It is of course possible that the license was issued under another name. The obituary of Samuel Gloyd that appeared in the Montgomery County *Sentinel* on July 12, 1878 does not mention the tavern, only that his occupation was the "cultivation of the soil" and that he had served as sheriff and constable of the county.

In 1879, Mrs. Rebecca A. Gloyd, the widow of Samuel Jr., built a warehouse in Gaithersburg. The town did business with her, mostly in the form of hiring her team for delivering lumber from the depot. Mrs. Gloyd was apparently a shrewd businesswoman, for on February 11, 1880, the town was presented with a bill from her in the amount of $1 for "the detention of her team at the depot for the day previous to the delivering of the lumber for the plank walk."

For a number of years the Gloyd property was the site of summer encampments of the National Guard. The *Sentinel* on May 5,1882 carried the announcement that the heirs of Samuel Gloyd had made a contract for the use of their land for this purpose and that the troops had been given permission to "cut down a large body of pines lying between the camp and the depot, and which obstructs the view from that point." It is further noted that "The troops will be accompanied by a fine band of thirty-two pieces and open air concerts at the Summit Hotel will no doubt add to the pleasure of the guests at this fashionable summer retreat." These encampments on the Gloyd property not only brought entertainment to the town but were instrumental in the establishment in 1884 of the Ayres Post Office at the railroad depot. This post office was named for Colonel R.B. Ayres, commander of the troops, and was opened for the convenience of the troops and the guests of the hotel.

Rebecca and Samuel's son Samuel Sylvester Gloyd went into business in Gaithersburg. He was born in 1841 and died in 1932. He married Ann Eliza Clements, daughter of Andrew and C. Ann (Howard) Clements in 1865, and they had eight children. In 1876, Samuel and Rebecca deeded 1.5 acres of land on the Frederick Road to Samuel Sylvester. This property had been purchased by them in 1860 from Edward Trail and was located across from the present Brookes Avenue. In 1878, Samuel S. Gloyd was a blacksmith, and in 1881, he opened a "green grocer shop" on this property. Gloyd served nine terms on the Gaithersburg Board of Commissioners and as its president in 1881. In that same year he was also a trustee for school no. 1 in the Gaithersburg district and was on the board of directors of the Baltimore Building and Loan and the Knoxville Southern Associations.

Another son, Edmund A. Gloyd, was born in 1863 and married Emily Arnold in 1895. He established his residence in Gaithersburg in 1920; prior to that he lived in Derwood. His son Edmund Russell Gloyd, born February 14, 1911, was an active citizen of Gaithersburg. While attending Gaithersburg High School, he was involved in efforts to produce a school paper and yearbook and became the first editor-in-chief of both. The *Blue and Gold*, established in 1928, and the *Sail On*, established in 1929, are still published by Gaithersburg High School. Edmund Russell Gloyd married Alice Virginia Walker in 1943 and had six children. Gloyd was a member of the Gaithersburg Lions Club for more than 32 years. He served on the Gaithersburg Bicentennial Coordinating Committee and compiled a pictorial history of bicentennial activities for the city archives. He also served as vice chairman of the Gaithersburg Charter Centennial Policy Commission and as their representative to the committee that compiled the history of Gaithersburg. From 1954 to 1959 he served on the Gaithersburg Town Council and the City Planning Commission and Board of Appeals.

THE DeSELLUM FAMILY

The town of Gaithersburg was formed from several tiny settlements, the oldest being Logtown at Summit Hall, which was established before 1770 and is home to the oldest structures in Gaithersburg. In 1806, James DeSellum and his wife, Catherine Fulks, daughter of Baltus and Sarah Fulks, bought her parents' 1-acre lot in Logtown. In 1828, James purchased 300 acres of Zoar from Thomas Beall's estate. He sold several parcels before his son and daughter, John T. and Sarah A. DeSellum, patented the remaining 251-acre estate as Summit Hall in 1857. This land was part of Zoar and other parcels and stretched from near Deer Park Road to just beyond the B&O tracks on Frederick Avenue.

The original Summit Hall farmhouse was a four-room log dwelling with a center hall. Logs still form the rear two rooms of the house but are exposed only in the interior basement stairwell. A two-room frame addition was built on the front of the house around 1857 and the residence has been updated several times since then. Nearby stands a chinked-log meat storehouse believed to be the oldest complete building in Gaithersburg.

John and his sister Sarah were slave owners, but they also expressed "unvarying devotion to the Union, Constitution and Government of the United States." In July of 1864, General Jubal Early's Confederate forces ravaged their farm, personal belongings, and livestock. According to anecdotal history the only thing the DeSellums had to show for the battle, aside from the devastation, was a glove left behind by General Early.

Both John T. and Sarah DeSellum were well educated but remained unmarried. They generously donated land at the corner of Summit Avenue for the Ascension Episcopal Church and other land on Summit Avenue for a public school. Later this property was the site of the Summit Hotel and, in 1925, was acquired for St. Martin's Roman Catholic Church and school.

John DeSellum informally divided the land on the west side of Frederick from Summit to Diamond Avenue in 1880 into 4-acre estate parcels that were largely developed with substantial frame Victorian houses by 1900. A further subdivision was created on two of these 4-acre parcels with other adjacent land in 1911 to create the Observatory Heights residential subdivision. The houses on the east side of the unit and the 100 block of South Frederick Avenue were built after 1911 on Observatory Heights lots. All of them are used today for light business or offices.

In 1886, John DeSellum sold the farm to his cousin Ignatius T. Fulks but retained a claim to the family graveyard and was buried there in 1891. Fulks decided to completely remodel Summit Hall in the new Victorian style and to add conveniences for his family of four children. Fulks later subdivided the land on Summit Avenue into Summit Park house lots that he sold and gave to his children and others. Two Fulks children's houses remain: the Severance House at 205 South Summit Avenue and the Thomas Iraneus Fulks house, built in 1897, at 208 South Frederick Avenue.

Fulks and his family operated the farm until 1931 when Ignatius T. Fulks died at age 99. The farm was sold in 1936 to Frank and Nettie Wilmot of Washington, D.C. In 1948, William H. Wilmot, son of Frank and Nettie, turned Summit Hall into the first scientifically grown sod turf farm in the United States. The grass grown at Summit Hall Farm was used at famous landmarks in Washington, D.C., including the U.S. Capitol, the

This is an early photograph of John T. DeSellum.

Lincoln Memorial, the White House, Arlington Cemetery, and many others. The popularity of the sod increased the volume of mail in the area and elevated the Gaithersburg Post Office to first-class status. To develop the popular grass, Wilmot worked with Frank Meyer of the University of Maryland, and together they made advances in agronomy at the farm in the mid-twentieth century.

In its early years, Summit Hall Farm played an important part in the community as the site of the first Gaithersburg School in 1859. In 1951, Gaithersburg High School was built on the site, where it still stands today, though much enlarged. The DeSellums donated part of the site for the Ascension Episcopal Church, the oldest remaining church in Gaithersburg. Another part of the site was leased to the United States Coast and Geodetic Survey, which built the Gaithersburg Latitude Observatory. The contributions from Summit Hall Farm remain a part of Gaithersburg today.

The City of Gaithersburg purchased the remaining 57.5 acres of the farm in 1982 and made good use of the land, which is now the home of Bohrer Park at Summit Hall Farm, named after longtime mayor W. Edward Bohrer Jr., who passed away in August 1998. Ed Bohrer was a lifetime Gaithersburg resident and the mayor from 1986 until his death at age 58. He was not only a great leader, but a good friend to many in the Gaithersburg community. Bohrer watched Gaithersburg grow from a small, rural, agricultural community to the booming city it is today. He was instrumental in shaping that growth and took pride in the fact that the citizens of Gaithersburg play such a strong role in the city's government.

Prior to his election as mayor, Ed Bohrer served on the Gaithersburg Planning Commission (1974–1978) and the Gaithersburg City Council (1976–1986). He was instrumental in beginning the anti-drug education program in city schools, the redesign of Olde Towne, the Wells/Robertson House Homeless Program, community policing, Council in the Communities, mixed-use zoning for neo-traditional development, the Smart Growth Initiative, new recreation programs and facilities such as the activity center, City Hall Concert Pavilion, Kentlands Mansion, Gaithersburg Upcounty Senior Center, the teen center, and the water park, and many more innovative programs and services.

THE DIAMOND FAMILY

William Craig Diamond was the first member of his family to come to the Gaithersburg area. He arrived some time prior to 1850, at which point he began living in the home of Francis C. Clopper. Both families were from Philadelphia. In 1853, Diamond's mother purchased 269 acres of Zoar and Resurvey on Younger Brother from the estate of Aaron Offutt. William built his home, which he called "Bellevue" on this property. After the death of his mother in 1864, he inherited all of these lands. Diamond invested part of his wealth in lots near the new railroad station and built the first new commercial building in Olde Towne in 1874, Diamond Hall. Both his farm and Bellevue remained in the family until 1957 when they became part of the site of the National Bureau of Standards. Diamond married Sarah Josephine Jenkins of Baltimore and had four children, but the only one to survive to adulthood was John Bernard Diamond, born March 25, 1857.

John B. Diamond grew up near Gaithersburg, attended local schools, and graduated from Rock Hill College in Ellicott City. He was an active farmer and businessman. His property consisted of Bellevue, Zoar (now the site of Watkins-Johnson on Quince Orchard Road), and "Cedarcroft," which was located on the present site of Weinschell Engineering Company on Clopper Road. He was also an investor in the First National Bank of Gaithersburg and served as its vice president until 1900. At that time he became president, and held that position until his death in 1926.

One of John B. Diamond's major business enterprises was the Gaithersburg Milling and Manufacturing Company, though he also operated the Summit Milling Company. Diamond was also an investor in the Summit Hotel corporation and later donated his interest in the property to the Catholic Church for the establishment of St. Martin's.

His name is perpetuated today in Gaithersburg by Diamond Avenue, one of the first four streets named by the newly incorporated town. On November 7, 1877, he married Grace Ranney of Delaware, Ohio, and they had five children: William, Eleanor, John Bernard Jr., Herbert, and Douglas.

William Carrell Diamond was the first child of John and Grace. He married Edith Vanderbilt and had two daughters, Doris and Louise. William Carrell was a graduate of Harvard Law School and practiced law in New York City.

The second of the five children born to John and Grace Diamond was Eleanor Ranney, who was born May 16,1880 and died July 21, 1881.

The third child was John Bernard Jr., who was born June 23, 1882 and died January 18, 1955. He married Laurie Beauregard, whose grandfather was General Pierre Gustav Toutant Beauregard, commander of the Confederate forces that opened the attack on Fort Sumter, South Carolina when the first shots of the Civil War were fired.

John B. Diamond Jr., better known as "Buck" Diamond, followed his father's example of participation in the political, business, and agricultural affairs of Gaithersburg and the county. He served as the treasurer of Montgomery County (1939–1948), as chief of the Montgomery County Revenue and Disbursement Division (1948–1952), as a member of the Montgomery County Board of Commissioners (1930–1934), and as the first police

Members of the Fulks and Severance families play parlor games in this photograph. (Courtesy of Betty Jeanne Jacobs.)

commissioner of the county. He was director and vice president of the Maryland/Virginia Milk Producers Association, president of the Montgomery County Farm Bureau, a charter member of the Upper Montgomery County Lions Club, and was active in other community and civic organizations. He also ran a dairy farm and, with his brothers, played on the local baseball team. He lived in the original Diamond home Bellevue.

The fourth child of John and Grace was Herbert Laurence, who was born August 15, 1884 and died December 5, 1961. Herb Diamond served as postmaster for the town of Gaithersburg from 1934 to 1937. After his father's death, he operated the Summit Milling Company. His home was at Cedarcroft. He married Marie Jones, and they had five children: John Bernard, Herbert Carvel, Grace Carrell (who died at the age of two), Eleanor, and Charles Benedict who married Margaret Nichol.

Douglas Byrnn, the fifth and last child of John and Grace, was born May 21, 1890 and died February 17, 1958. He and his wife, Gladys Wheeler, had two children: Nancy, who married John Darby Bowman and had children Darby, Douglas, David, and Peter; and William, who married Martha Eisele and had children Craig, Douglas, Kathleen, and Joan. Gladys died in 1932, and Douglas Sr. married Carroll Martin in 1939.

Like the other members of his family, Douglas Byrnn Diamond was active in community affairs but his first love was his dairy farm, which he operated on the Zoar property. When Pearl Harbor was attacked in 1941, he was called upon to set up an air raid alert station at the firehouse. Douglas accomplished this within 24 hours and manned the first night's watch himself. He was the star pitcher of the local baseball team and played on the team at Georgetown Preparatory School. Douglas was also active in the Maryland/Virginia Milk Producers Association and the Lions Club. He was one of the organizers of the Gaithersburg–Washington Grove Fire Department and served as its president from 1937 to 1938. He died in 2001.

3. COMMERCIAL DEVELOPMENT

The Brookes family's land was first developed on the west side of Frederick Road. The corner of Chestnut Street and Frederick Avenue, now occupied by a tire store at 126 Frederick Avenue, has been a commercial site since 1815. The remainder of the north end of Gaithersburg was primarily in agricultural use until the twentieth century with a few properties fronting on Frederick sold as residential lots in the late nineteenth century.

This early commercial site is part of "Resurvey of Valentine's Garden, Enlarged," a portion of the 786-acre tract conveyed by Martha Brookes and her son James B. Brookes to Samuel Funk of Washington County.

In 1815, Samuel Funk sold 6 acres from the Resurvey on Valentine's Garden Enlarged tract for $100 to Robert Crawford. According to Scharf's *History of Western Maryland*, Crawford was the first tavern or innkeeper in Gaithersburg and was there by 1815. His tavern and public house provided food and lodging to travelers along the Great Road. In 1826, Crawford sold the 6 acres to John P. Stewart for $1,250.

Stewart married Elizabeth Gloyd of Gaithersburg. She was the daughter of Samuel and Jane Sibley Gloyd of Logtown. It is not known whether the Stewarts continued operating the property as a tavern, leased it to others, or changed its use entirely. Elizabeth Stewart was postmistress of the Middlebrook Mills Post Office from 1833 to 1846, so presumably she was not living in Gaithersburg during that time.

The widowed Elizabeth Stewart and her children sold the 6 acres to Catherine and Eli Burriss for $300 in 1851. Catherine Burriss was a daughter of John and Elizabeth Stewart.

Early in his life Eli Burriss was a farmer, but later records show that he took up the trade of carpentry. He died in 1889 and is buried with Catherine, who died in 1895, at St. Rose's Cemetery. Catherine's obituary in the *Sentinel* stated that she was one of the original inhabitants of Gaithersburg. Reuben Burriss was one of her seven children.

An 1878 map of Gaithersburg shows a building at the corner of Chestnut Street and Frederick Avenue labeled "Eli Burriss, B. S. Sh." (blacksmith shop), with the notation "J.A. Burriss." This presumably was John A. Burriss's blacksmith shop. The town minutes of September 14, 1914 state that the town clerk was to notify John Burris that he must secure a permit for the new building he was erecting. Burris died in 1918.

In 1901, Robert A. and Rosa Young acquired the corner property in two parcels. The first was the house lot. The other lot of 16,401 square feet was conveyed from Nathan and Hattie A. Cooke, who had acquired it from Catherine A. Burriss in 1891.

Robert A. Young and, later, his son Robert L. Young operated a store in a two-and-a-half story, narrow and deep brick building at the corner of Frederick Avenue and Chestnut Street. Kim Walker recalled going to the store as a child in the 1930s and 1940s, particularly before Christmas, when Young would have children's toys and bicycles arrayed on the third story. The first floor housed a grocery store and the second displayed work clothes. Young and his mother lived in a house next to the store that was set back from Frederick Avenue. Mrs. Young could often be seen, into her 90s, on the porch in her rocking chair in the middle of summer wrapped up in a blanket.

Nathan J. Walker's Rolling Knoll Farm extended down both sides of Goshen Road into Olde Towne Gaithersburg. It was later a dairy farm owned by Nathan's son McKendree Walker and his sons Grover and W. Ralph Walker. Nathan's other sons also owned farms in the area. The eldest, John Wesley Walker, owned the Gaither farm, which was sold to the Asbury Methodist Home. George Edward Walker owned a farm west of his father's Rolling Knoll that is now part of Montgomery Village. James King Walker owned a farm on the east side of Goshen Road that included the Spring Valley Mill. This is also part of Montgomery Village.

In 1961, Ralph and Grover Walker sold the 412-acre Rolling Knoll Farm to Barbara Walker and Milton Kettler. Barbara Walker Kettler was the daughter of merchant J. Forest and Rosa Walker, and cousin to farmers Grover and Ralph Walker. The farm became the first section of Montgomery Village. The Kettler brothers purchased other adjacent farms and land in the area to build the new community. The houses that were later removed for the Lakeforest regional shopping center and its adjacent commercial area included the home of the late Mayor Bohrer's family, among others.

South Gaithersburg and Mount Pleasant

The southern end of today's Gaithersburg was composed of large family farms until the 1960s. Known as Mount Pleasant, this area covered the west side of South Frederick Avenue from Deer Park Road to Shady Grove Road. It belonged to Colonel Zadock Magruder before 1800 and later to his son and heir Robert Pottinger Magruder. It was sold in 1838 by Robert Magruder's estate to Lemuel Clements. The Clements family and Eugene B. Casey kept most of this property in large tracts until 1945.

A house called Mount Pleasant is said to have been built by Colonel Magruder near the intersection of the present Shady Grove Road and South Frederick Avenue about 1807.

The Magruder family arrived in Maryland in 1652 when Alexander Magruder was deported from Scotland as an indentured servant following the Scottish Rebellion. His son John Magruder of Dunblane, Prince George's County, obtained three or more grants of land between 1736 and 1766. John Magruder's son Zadok, the first to reside in Montgomery County, inherited 600 acres in 1745 and built the Ridge at Redlands.

Zadock Magruder (1745–1811) was the third-generation Magruder in Maryland, a grandson of Alexander Magruder. Colonel Zadok Magruder attained his rank in command of the Home Defense Battalion of Lower Frederick County during the Revolutionary War. He was appointed, along with his brother Nathan, to a commission to establish and organize Montgomery County in 1776.

Colonel Magruder's son Robert Pottinger Magruder was a planter and was involved in the early government, serving in the Maryland House of Delegates in 1799, 1800, and 1801. A brick house such as Mount Pleasant would have been appropriate to his station in life. After his father's death, Robert P. Magruder owned and operated the farm until Mount Pleasant and 437 acres of land were sold to Lemuel Clements.

Clements was born to Henry and Jane Clements in 1794 and was a well-traveled adventurer before settling down in his native Montgomery County. He made one horseback trip to Fort Dearborn (Chicago) at age 22 and another trip to St. Louis, returning via Louisville, Kentucky. There he met George M. Bibb, a Marylander by birth, and their friendship lasted for the remainder of their lives.

Bibb was a graduate of Princeton, had been admitted to the bar of Kentucky, and was on the Supreme Court of that state. He was in the U.S. Senate for three terms, one of them as a colleague of Henry Clay, and in 1844, he became secretary of the treasury under John Tyler. Judge Bibb practiced law in Washington and lived in Georgetown.

Bibb set up a summer home in Gaithersburg near his protégé Lemuel Clements and probably as an investment, since the proposed B&O Metropolitan Branch line from Washington, D.C. to Point of Rocks and west would go through his property. His holdings stretched from Brown's Station on Clopper Road to the B&O tracks at Diamond Avenue in Gaithersburg and included the Meem farm and fair grounds along the present Chestnut Street.

Martenet and Bond's 1865 "Map of Montgomery County, Maryland" shows "L. Clements" or "John Ambrose Clements" on four farmsteads along Frederick Avenue from the Muddy Branch to what is now Shady Grove Road.

Lemuel Clements died November 1, 1880. His sons and heirs from his first marriage inherited property on the east side of Frederick Avenue. Mary Elizabeth Clements,

Eugene B. Casey purchased Mount Pleasant Farm and the Casey Barn, which was built in 1938.

33

daughter from his second marriage, inherited Mount Pleasant and 180 acres of land on the west side of Frederick Avenue. Her family operated this farm until the death of her husband, Lee Offutt, in 1929. Roger Brookes Farquhar described the house about 1950.

> Driving from Washington to Frederick, one's attention is attracted to an old brick house to the left of the highway four miles beyond Rockville. It has every appearance of age in design and detail. Its situation commands a sweeping view for many miles toward the north and west.
>
> The Mt. Pleasant house stands on a high knoll facing the east. Many years ago the ancient Braddock's Trail passed directly in front and close to the house. The front hall leads through a door to a rear yard. A large room on the right is a parlor with a fireplace, and the room on the left a dining room with a large fireplace. This interesting old place has been owned for many years by Eugene Casey, local investor.

Local businessman Eugene B. Casey purchased Mount Pleasant and the farm. Casey Barn was built in 1938 as a dairy barn, but it has had a secondary life as a signboard, most notably for political candidates in the 1940s. This started with E. Russell Gloyd of Gaithersburg, who painted the exterior of the barn as a campaign sign for Franklin D. Roosevelt in 1940 and then took photographs of the finished product. The dairy barn soon became a local landmark.

According to an interview with Eugene Casey in the *Frederick Post*, all the lumber to build the barn came from Casey's two Clements farms that were located across from one another on Frederick Avenue. Raymond Moore of Washington designed the barn from Casey's general plan. The concrete blocks used for the first level were purchased in Frederick County. The second story is frame.

The 60 cows at the dairy barn produced 300 gallons of milk daily, which were sold to the Thompson and Chestnut Farms dairies. In 1971, Eugene Casey deeded the barn and land to the City of Gaithersburg for use as a community center.

The Gaithersburg Community Center is an outstanding example of the city's ability to appreciate its past while also adapting it to future needs. The community center renovation was funded through a state open space community development block grant and through city funds. An aggressive fund-raising drive in 1977 and 1978 raised money for equipment through outright donations and a community rummage sale. The barn was ready in the fall of 1977 and the formal dedication ceremony took place in November.

The center was an immediate success. The City Recreation Guide for spring 1978 showed an average of 35 to 40 groups using the center each month, and the activity has not diminished. In the mid-1990s, records showed that approximately 9,000 people used the Casey Community Center each month.

MUDTOWN

The area where Muddy Branch crosses the Frederick Road was designated on John J. Abert's 1838 "Routes for the Proposed Maryland Canal" map as Mudtown. Gaithersburg

This photograph shows the Casey Barn as it appeared before a political rally in 1940. (Courtesy of E. Russell Gloyd.)

is the next name along the Frederick Road. Obviously Mudtown was inhabited at the time, but by whom is unknown. It was largely undeveloped until after Lemuel Clements's death in 1880. The *Sentinel* of March 18, 1881 carried notices of an estate sale of 110 acres of his property. "The Branch Farm" was to be sold at auction on April 6, 1881 to the highest bidder. The property was described as follows:

> Located on the public road leading from Georgetown to Frederick, four miles from Rockville and one mile from Gaithersburg, and within one hundred yards of the Washington Grove Station . . . and adjoins the lands of John Ambrose Clements, and William R. Easton.
>
> This land is well wooded and watered, under good enclosure, and has a good apple orchard on it. The buildings consist of a comfortable Log Dwelling, stable, Corn House, and other accessory outbuildings. The good natural quality of the soil, and the location of this farm, being almost immediately online of the Metropolitan Railroad and its proximity to the thriving town of Gaithersburg, render it desirable property.

SOUTH FREDERICK AVENUE

In 1780, John Bruce, presumed to be an heir of Williamson Bruce, conveyed 229.5 acres (the southern half) of Deer Park to William Holmes for £12,000. In 1783, the Deer Park tract was assessed at £12,229. It consisted of one log dwelling, one tobacco house, 90 cleared acres, and 3 acres marsh, and was one of four properties owned by William Holmes. In 1790, he owned 30 slaves, but it is not known at which of his properties they lived. In 1793, the 229-acre tract was assessed at about £226. Holmes served in the Maryland House of Delegates in 1786, was judge of the orphans' court from 1802 to 1803, and was associate judge of the circuit court in 1803. He died in 1825 at nearly 79 years of age. His son Richard, born in 1791, inherited the Deer Park tract.

In 1860, during a depression and on the eve of the Civil War, Francis Clopper bought the property from Newland and Sarah Irish. He did not live in Gaithersburg but at "The Woodlands" on Clopper's Road. The southern half of the Deer Park tract that he purchased was on both sides of the preferred route for the proposed Metropolitan Railroad and surrounded the intersection of Laytonsville and Goshen Roads. Clopper stood to profit handsomely from development of this land when the railroad went through. Although he and his partners lost their charter to build the Metropolitan Railroad, they were able to persuade the B&O to build the new line following their surveyed route through Montgomery County and Gaithersburg. Clopper did not require the B&O to condemn his Deer Park land for the new line's tracks in 1868. He deeded property to the B&O for a nominal sum plus an agreement that the B&O would construct a station and turnout siding on his property.

Francis Clopper died December 31, 1868 having survived his wife, Jane Byrne, who had died in 1865. Mary Augusta Hutton, wife of William Rich Hutton, and William Douglas Clopper and his wife, Mary Sophia, were Francis Clopper's heirs.

Mrs. Hutton's husband, William Rich Hutton, was an engineer of world renown. They married in 1855. Hutton served as assistant engineer under Captain Montgomery Meigs in the building of the Washington Aqueduct and Cabin John Bridge, as chief engineer of the Annapolis waterworks and the Chesapeake and Ohio Canal, as consulting engineer for the Croton Aqueduct in New York, and as chief engineer for the Washington Bridge over the Harlem River and the Hudson Tunnel in New York. He was awarded the diploma of the Paris Exposition of 1878 for his design of locks for the Kanawha Canal. Hutton also provided the design for the second church building of the St. Rose of Lima mission in 1884 after the original church was destroyed by fire. Mr. and Mrs. Hutton owned a large part of the downtown Gaithersburg area around the rail station and City Hall, as well as the large Clopper tract west of Gaithersburg overlooking Seneca Creek, which she inherited from her parents.

At the death of Douglas Clopper, his other heirs and Mary Augusta Hutton partitioned the real estate that had been left from Francis Clopper's estate. Mary Augusta Hutton and others got all of Francis Clopper's 229.5-acre Deer Park estate.

The Clopper/Hutton holdings encompassed most of the land in Olde Towne east of Summit Avenue to Washington Grove and were bounded by Deer Park Road back to Frederick Avenue and down Summit. They include such sites as the B&O Railroad Station, the Wells-Robertson House, City Hall, and the present Deer Park community neighborhood. The Huttons started selling lots from their Deer Park holdings in 1877. The new construction was entirely residential until one business, Becraft's, was approved in 1947. The area remained residential until the 1960s when the Holbrook Center at 411 South Frederick Avenue was constructed.

LOGTOWN AND SUMMIT HALL

The land patented in 1857 as Summit Hall encompassed the west side of Frederick Avenue from Deer Park Road to Diamond Avenue and included the triangle of land between Summit, Frederick Avenue, and the railroad. Before it was Summit Hall it was part of a larger holding owned by the Briscoe family at Zoar on Quince Orchard Road.

Gerard Briscoe, who platted "Germansburgh," or Logtown, was a justice of the county and levy courts from 1777 to 1778. He moved to Virginia before 1789 but continued to speculate in real estate in the Gaithersburg area. He and his father, Robert, amassed land and patented it as Zoar in 1793. Zoar totaled 1,238 acres, embracing several earlier grants.

SUMMIT HALL SMOKE HOUSE

This outbuilding on the ridge of Summit Hall Farm is treasured as the oldest complete historic structure within the City of Gaithersburg. Historically known as the smoke house, its notched logs and chinked mortar serve as a modern-day reminder of the early

Francis Cassat Clopper was instrumental in the development of Montgomery County. This 1810 portrait was made by Thomas Sully. (Courtesy of Helen C. Madine.)

settlement of Logtown. The City of Gaithersburg commissioned Dell Corporation in 1990 to make restorative repairs to this important historic landmark.

Approximately 14 feet square, the building rests on a fieldstone base. The roof was originally covered with rough wood shakes, which have been replaced with composition shingles. The purloins and ridgepole have also been replaced with modern lumber and plywood sheathing.

The short wide door on the east facade is made from three wide planks nailed to two interior horizontal members. The door was originally designed with a loop leather and peg salt-resistant iron hinge system but is presently mounted with wide triangular iron strap hinges. A concrete floor has been added to the interior of the smokehouse but the center section can be removed to expose the original fire pit.

THE GEORGE GLOYD HOUSE

In 1915, Ignatius Fulks gave his son Oscar a nearly 1-acre, L-shaped lot that wrapped behind Ascension Church from Summit to Frederick Avenues. Oscar built his home

The Summit Hall smoke house is the oldest building in Gaithersburg. This photograph of Zoe Wilmot, Frances Wilmot Kellerman, and Lloyd Miller was taken in 1936.

facing South Summit Avenue and the property that fronted on Frederick Avenue remained vacant. In 1930, Oscar Fulks, his wife, Edith, and his father sold the portion that fronted onto Frederick Avenue to George Andrew Gloyd Sr. and his wife, Alice.

George Gloyd was a state policeman and a builder and contractor born in Gaithersburg on April 21, 1867. His contracting firm of Gloyd and Kingsley built City Hall and the Dosh Stables on East Diamond. He married Alice Wallach on November 5, 1902, and they had six children. One of their sons was Carlton Andrew Gloyd who reassembled the Gloyd tract that was sold to the Chesapeake and Potomac Telephone Co. of Maryland (C&P).

George Gloyd died in 1942 and Alice sold the house to George L. and Ethel M. Osterwise in 1950. Dr. Osterwise was the principal of Gaithersburg High School, then located on North Summit Avenue. In 1960, the Osterwises sold the house to Arvella Royal Bryant. Bryant bought the Blue Fountain Inn, a popular Rockville restaurant at College Avenue and Route 355 and operated it as Le Fontain Bleu until it was destroyed by fire.

Another Gaithersburg house built on Ignatius Fulks's property is the Fulks-Harding house at 20 South Summit Avenue. In 1903, Ignatius T. Fulks received a building permit for this vernacular two-story house in Fulks Woods between the Summit Hotel and the railroad. It may have been used as a rental house connected with the hotel or the school that occupied the hotel in the winter. For many years it was the family home of William Harding and his family.

Harding worked for the B&O Railroad at various stations along the Metropolitan Line and for a time was the operator at the telegraph station near Owen's Crossing at Frederick and Diamond Avenues. Then he became the crossing guard at the Summit Avenue station. Two years after his retirement an express passenger train came through town at a high speed one foggy February evening. It struck a car crossing the tracks killing Harding's son Delbert, his daughter, her husband, and other members of her family. The flagman that took Mr. Harding's job had gone off duty for the night. It was this tragedy that finally got automatic signals for the Gaithersburg crossing rather than a flagman, but it came at a high price. The house later became the home and office of Dr. Walter Kaplan and his wife, Benita. It was listed as a Gaithersburg historic site in 2000.

THE OBSERVATORY

On the highest point of Summit Hall Farm in Gaithersburg, beyond the original Observatory Heights houses on the West End of DeSellum Avenue, stands a small white frame building ornamented with a star over its door. About 200 feet to the south is a white meridian mark pier, or azimuth marker, used to align a telescope. There are five in-ground monuments establishing geographic latitude and longitude, elevation above sea level, and the direction of the magnetic north pole. This is the United States Coast and Geodetic Survey's first observatory for the study of the variation of latitude, built by Edwin Smith in Gaithersburg in 1899 after he had made beginning studies on this subject from his home in Rockville. The observatory represented a certain triumph in obtaining official recognition of work that the astronomer Smith had begun earlier on a volunteer basis.

In 1889, when the phenomenon of the Earth's wobble on its axis was first discovered and announced, the International Geodetic Association began a search for strategic

Edwin Smith sits on the porch of the Gaithersburg Latitude Observatory's caretaker house in 1900. (Photo by E.G. Fischer.)

locations for stations to carry out systematic observations to solve this scientific puzzle. The association, with central headquarters in Potsdam, Germany, was supported by the most prominent nations of the world including the United States and the majority of the governments of Europe.

The superintendent's report of 1898–1899 shows that an agreement was reached by members of the International Geodetic Association to establish five observatories near the parallel of 39° 08' north latitude. They were spaced as evenly as possible around the Northern Hemisphere in the United States, Russia, Japan, and Italy.

The site selection process for station locations included stringent tests of social, hygienic, seismological, and meteorological conditions. The prime requisites were that each station must be near the 39th parallel and have a fair proportion of clear nights throughout the year. The first four stations selected were Mizusawa, Japan; Carloforte, Italy; Gaithersburg, Maryland; and Ukiah, California. Later, stations in Tschardjui, Russia and Cincinnati, Ohio were added.

In 1898, Edwin Smith received official encouragement and funds from the International Geodetic Association, which he used to begin work at Summit Hall Farm. The work at the Gaithersburg and Ukiah stations was supervised by the Coast and Geodetic Survey's International Polar Motion Service program. Smith set up the observatory in ten days and began observations on October 18, 1899.

Four identical Zenith telescopes were constructed by Julius Wanschaff in Berlin for the four new stations. At Gaithersburg, the telescope was deep-mounted on a pedestal with a bedrock base to eliminate vibrations. The 6-foot, 6-inch sliding roof allowed the large telescope to view the skies.

"Mr. Astronomer Smith," as he was called locally, made his observations on a volunteer basis during his free evenings. He missed his family in Rockville, however, so he installed a telephone in the observatory. He built a little cottage by the observatory, heated with a wood burning stove. One large room served as the office, the housekeeper had one bedroom, and his family the other. He would often bring his children up two at a time and even allow them to look through the telescope. When entertaining, he sometimes would hire a horse-drawn bus and drive his party from Rockville to Gaithersburg to look at the heavens. Among his various accomplishments was the establishment of the first longitude net around the Earth. Smith gave the task of regular observations to another astronomer in 1901, but he remained interested in the project until his death in 1912.

The six observatories around the world worked in close concert. Twelve groups of stars, each containing six pairs at small distances not exceeding 24 degrees and two pairs at great distances of 60 degrees were selected. Two groups of stars were observed each night at each station in accordance with a schedule of dates, times, and durations from 1900 until 1914 when the economic constraints of World War I forced the closing of the Gaithersburg and Cincinnati stations. Gaithersburg resumed operations in 1932.

Smith's original office was moved and converted into a residence for the observer. In 1911, a building was shown attached to the observatory to house the first Zenith tube telescope, which photographed the stars. In 1948, the observer's house was replaced with a new brick residence and the original office was sold to John H. Walker and moved to Cedar Avenue. It can be identified by its "eyebrow" windows.

Alfred Helm took over from Earl Williams in 1957 and worked as observer until the 1970s. In 1968, representatives of the Japanese Embassy presented a gift of bells from the city's sister observatory in Mizusawa to Helm and Mayor Harold Morris. In an earlier letter, the mayor of Mizusawa proposed a friendship between Gaithersburg and Mizusawa, "both as the cities of international scientific research work and to promote it with our good will, which would be the greatest honour and joy for me."

Mac Currin, who was an assistant to Alfred Helm, was the last observer at Gaithersburg when the observatory closed in 1982. The National Oceanic and Atmospheric Administration computerized the 90-year-old star tracking system and the Zenith telescope was moved to storage. The City of Gaithersburg acquired the abandoned observatory from the federal government on May 31, 1987 under the Historic Monuments Program. The City hired Dell Corporation to repair and restore the observatory building, and during Preservation Week in May 1990, a special dedication was held at the observatory honoring the internationally significant site as the city's first National Scientific Landmark. This designation included the observatory, the meridian marker, and the five in-ground Coast and Geodetic Survey markers. The observatory was unveiled for the first time since restoration, and the old Zenith telescope was returned to its pedestal for this special occasion.

SUMMIT PARK AND OBSERVATORY HEIGHTS

In the early 1880s, John T. DeSellum informally subdivided his property north of Summit Avenue on the west side of South Frederick Avenue into 4-acre estate lots. The first lots were sold to Eliza and Philemon Smith and members of the Lodge family. Ignatius T. Fulks later purchased Summit Hall Farm and the remaining unsold estate parcels in 1886 and laid out an unrecorded residential building lot subdivision called Summit Park between DeSellum and Summit Avenues in 1893.

In 1911, two of the estate parcels and adjacent land owned by the heirs of Eliza and Philemon Smith were sold to Charles Brinkerhoff and subdivided into 76 building lots called Observatory Heights after the astronomical observatory built on DeSellum Avenue in 1899. The entire area between the railroad tracks and Summit Avenue on the west side of Frederick is now generally characterized as Observatory Heights. A number of the original Summit Park and estate houses remain on Frederick Avenue.

THE T.I. FULKS HOUSE

Thomas Iraneus Fulks and his wife, Frances, built this classic Queen Anne Victorian house in 1897 on Summit Park land purchased from his parents. T.I. Fulks was the great-grandson of Baltus Fulks, one of the first Logtown settlers. The house has been designated a local historic site for its association with the Fulks family but also as an outstanding example of late-nineteenth-century architecture. Outstanding features include a patterned slate roof with terra cotta crests and a square tower. Thomas Fulks was a successful businessman and farmer who was also active in local politics and community affairs. He served on the town council from 1898 to 1906.

In 1919, T.I. Fulks sold the property in two parcels to Thaddeus T. and Ann P. Bussard, who had retired from farming. Their farm is now a well-known historical site, the Montgomery County Agricultural Farm Park. The Bussard family owned the property through several generations until it was sold to Robert J. and Marilyn Wilson. Dr. Robert J. Wilson is a dentist and the son of Dr. Herman Wilson, the first administrator of Asbury Methodist Home.

THE GAITHER PROPERTY AND "SELF PRESERVATION"

The dividing line between the north and south portions of Deer Park is slightly north of today's Diamond Avenue. In 1779, Charles Bruce sold the 229-acre northern half to Thomas Cowley of Anne Arundel County for £6,000. Two years later, Cooley sold it to Jesse Wilcoxen, who then sold the property for £500 to Henry Brookes before 1793. Brookes may have obtained it as marriage dower for his daughter Margaret, who married Benjamin Gaither. By 1797, the 229 acres of Deer Park land were assessed to Benjamin Gaither, but title remained with Henry Brookes.

Sometime before 1802 it was discovered that a small triangular sliver of unpatented and unclaimed land lay between Deer Park and the adjacent tracts Robert's Delight and Younger Brother. This 3-acre parcel had approximately 110 feet of frontage on Frederick

Avenue and extended 1,500 feet to Summit Avenue along the north side and in the right-of-way of the present Diamond Avenue. By 1802, it was probably being used as part of the Brookes/property and controlled access to all future lots fronting on Diamond Avenue. It was a small but extremely valuable piece of land. Benjamin Gaither patented this 3-acre parcel in his own name in 1802 as "Self Preservation."

It is likely this Self Preservation patent date that inspired the story that Benjamin Gaither built the first house in Gaithersburg in 1802. In fact, the Gaither family was probably living in this location prior to the patenting of Self Preservation as Benjamin was paying taxes on the land in 1797 and their first child, Bushrod Washington Gaither, was born in 1800.

Although the precise date of his settlement is not known, it is certainly true that Benjamin Gaither built his home, blacksmith shop, and a tavern and store on the Self Preservation/Deer Park corner. He farmed the Deer Park land where Brookes, Walker, and Russell Avenues are located. He had an extensive household and owned 11 slaves in 1824, when his assets were placed in a trusteeship to guarantee a debt to his son William.

Benjamin Gaither was plagued by economic problems throughout his life. He was declared insolvent in 1828 and again his property was placed in trust. A few years after Gaither's death in 1838, his wife and daughters sold 54.75 acres of Deer Park to Samuel

The Forest Oak tree was felled by a 1997 storm.

Gloyd Jr. and his wife, Rebecca, in 1844. The house on this property near the Forest Oak tree was known in subsequent years as "The Gloyd Mansion" and was credited by local anecdotal history as incorporating the original log Benjamin Gaither house. It was remodeled in the late nineteenth century with a more fashionable two-story double bay façade, which put it in the same class as the owners of Summit Hall and the Meem family on Chestnut Street. Over the years the structure served many functions besides a home. It became a temporary hospital for wounded soldiers during the Civil War and a location for Roman Catholics to celebrate Mass in Gaithersburg before St. Martin's Church was established. The house and tree had become local landmarks by the mid-nineteenth century.

Carlton Gloyd acquired four pieces of land in the Deer Park tract between 1941 and 1957 that had been in the Samuel Gloyd estate, including the property and house at 5 North Frederick Avenue. In 1957, having reassembled a good portion of his family's home property, Carlton Gloyd sold 3.5865 acres of his "Carlton Gloyd Tract" to the C&P Telephone Co. The house was torn down and the new switching station of the C&P was built on the site. It is still used for communication service by Verizon.

The last tangible link to the town founders Benjamin Gaither, Margaret Brookes Gaither, and the Gloyd family came down in June 1997 when a summer storm toppled the nearly 300-year-old Forest Oak tree. The loss was deeply felt and most of the wood from the tree was distributed to the community. Several large pieces were salvaged by the City to make into commemorative plaques, and the Forest Oak marker was removed.

Carson Ward is second from the right in this early twentieth-century photograph of his store.

RUSSELL AND BROOKES ADDITION

Rebecca Gloyd sold a major portion of her 54 acres of undeveloped land to Reister Russell, who allied with Thomas B. Brookes to subdivide and plat the Russell and Brookes Addition to Gaithersburg in 1888. Russell and Brookes were descendants of Henry Brookes and were related to the Gaither family.

Thomas B. Brookes purchased an undivided equal interest in the subdivision in 1892 from Lee M. and Sallie L. Lipscombe, Henry and Rosa Miller, and John B. and Grace Diamond. These individuals were all entrepreneurs and real estate investors in Gaithersburg. In 1926, George H. and Edith S. Lamar bought lots 1, 2, 3, and 4, block 1, of the Russell and Brookes Addition at a public sale for $9,000 from the holders of a deed of trust. They sold it the next year to Buell M. Gardner and his wife. The building at 17 North Frederick is one-half of a building that was about 40 feet wide when built in 1924. The south half and an addition were removed by permit in 1969.

Kim Walker remembered that in the 1930s and 1940s the building housed Calloway's Restaurant, which was next door to the Lyric movie theatre. Many drunks hung out under the railroad overpass bridge across from Calloway's and frightened small children on their way home from the movies, she said. Calloway's later moved out to the east side of North Frederick Avenue slightly past where Odend'Hal Avenue is now located.

In the 1960s, Calloway's former site at 17 North Frederick housed an arcade with pinball games and ice cream. That business was closed because it attracted a drug trade. Also in the 1960s, it housed the Franklin Press business of Alfred and Merton Duvall, descendants of the Duvalls who had their blacksmith shop at 211 North Frederick, where the Duvall Center is now located. Merton Duvall later served as mayor of Gaithersburg.

CARSON WARD'S STORE

Carson Ward opened his dry goods and general merchandise store at 101 North Frederick Avenue after the 1890 death of his father Henry Clay Ward of Ward and Fulks. Carson Ward was mayor of Gaithersburg from 1904 to 1906 and was elected to several terms on the town council. He served in the Maryland legislature from 1921 to 1924. The Carson Ward store served as town hall in 1912, and the Jefferson Literary Club established a library for public use on the second story.

It also served as the first meeting place of Forest Oak Lodge no. 123 of the Knights of Pythias and the Pentalpha Lodge no. 194 Masonic Lodge before these organizations acquired separate quarters. It has been extensively rebuilt and remodeled by the owner, Mattress Discounters, but care was taken to preserve the familiar form and appearance of the building.

JAMES B. GAITHER HOUSE

The land at 215 North Frederick Avenue is part of the Margaret Brookes/Benjamin Gaither property left to their two daughters, Martha and Eveline. As Benjamin Gaither seemed to have constant financial difficulties, his sons did not have land as patrimony.

Martha Gaither, daughter of Benjamin, remained single. Her sister Eveline married Moses P. Hughes but, according to the divorce proceedings filed in November 1853, they lived together only 18 months. Under the provisions of their grandfather Henry Brookes's will, Eveline and Martha inherited the Deer Park land at their mother Margaret's death. However, in a deed dated March 2 1833, Margaret, Martha, and Eveline Gaither transferred the property to Beall Gaither, another brother of Martha, Eveline, and James B. Gaither. Martha and Eveline came back into possession of the land in 1844 when Beall and his wife, Eliza, conveyed it back to them. When their brother James B. Gaither married Virginia Cecil in 1861, the sisters were living on the part of Deer Park where the old Asbury home now stands. It is highly probable that they were living there as early as 1850.

This property was at the center of several scandals and lawsuits involving James B. Gaither, his sister Eveline, his first wife's grandniece, and his spouses. The lot is part of the land that Gaither obtained from his sister Eveline prior to his first marriage in 1861 to his cousin Virginia. The intent, as stated by Eveline, was to transfer the land to a third party and then back to Eveline to produce a clear title to her. Eveline agreed and stated that she signed the documents without reading them. Evidently, the property was transferred to James B. Gaither.

In 1866, Gaither purchased the same 15 acres from his sisters to build his house. Four months later he transferred it to his wife, Virginia. In 1868, he bought an additional 11 acres from his sisters adjoining the 15 acres, and in 1870, on the same day he recorded the 1868 deed, he also recorded the transfer of the second parcel to his wife. Virginia died in 1878 and left everything, including the two parcels described above as well as other land, to her husband.

During the marriage of James B. Gaither to Virginia, her grandniece Emily Cecil came to live with them. She was 20 years old at the time of Virginia's death, while Gaither was 63. On June 12, 1879, he deeded to Emily Cecil "for love and affection and the devoted attention to me by the niece of my late wife" the two adjoining parcels on Frederick Road and all the china, silver, and household and kitchen furnishings. However, he reserved the use of all of the property to himself for the term of his natural life. He did deed other property to her. One week later he married Susanna V. Brookes, widow of another cousin of James B. and Virginia Gaither.

In 1880, Emily Cecil married James E. Rabbitt, and in 1883, she sued Gaither for fraud for tricking her into turning back over to him the property that he had conveyed to her. After a sensational trial, the equity court returned the property on Frederick Avenue to Emily Cecil Rabbitt.

But Gaither's troubles were not over yet. In 1884, Susanna V. Gaither sued him for divorce on grounds of cruelty, including holding drunken parties and trying to harm her by keeping her in an unheated room while she was sick. James B. Gaither died on February 19, 1885, and Susanna sued in March 1885 to assert her dower rights over the property that he had inherited from his wife Virginia but which he had sold, borrowed on, or left to others in his will.

Susanna was successful, and among other property awarded her were 3 acres of the parcel at no. 215, presumably including the James B. Gaither house. Susanna V. Gaither was the mother of Thomas B. Brookes, who inherited much of the land now occupied by

This is an early photograph of the inside of Carson Ward's store.

the Brookes and Russell Subdivision. Susanna lived at 16 Brookes Avenue at one time, and then with her son at Redlands in her later years. She died in 1903.

Apparently Susanna received a life estate only, since the next transfer of the property in 1919 is between the heirs of Emily Cecil, who died in 1886. Joseph C. and Bertha Rabbitt transferred their interest in the 26 acres to Joseph's brother John O. Rabbitt, and in 1920, John O. and Agnes C. Rabbitt transferred the land to Charles Herman Rabbitt. The deed notes that this land is the same as that conveyed by James B. Gaither to Emily Cecil, that Emily Cecil had died intestate, her sole heirs being her husband (deceased) and her two sons.

The land was part of the parcel sold by Charles Herman Rabbitt to Gaithersburg Realty in 1920. The old house and lot changed hands rapidly until Willie Neal Hurley and others acquired it in 1948. The Hurleys sold it in 1960 to Farmers Banking and Trust, which by merger became the First National Bank of Maryland. The house was razed for a two-story bank building.

4. The Civil War

The Civil War divided the United States and Gaithersburg, and the longevity of the dissension and the bitter feelings that resulted were deep. The war had profound and long-lasting social effects in Gaithersburg. For a while in the mid-nineteenth century, the town even had two names, two Methodist churches, and duplicates of several social organizations. Reconciliation did not occur until the 1940s.

Civil War Action in Montgomery County

For four long years from 1861 to 1865, huge armies criss-crossed the South and the border states, including Maryland. It was not until the mid-twentieth century brought an influx of newcomers that the war and its aftermath retreated from public consciousness and the raw wounds healed.

But in the 1850s the possibility of secession was very much on the minds of Gaithersburg's citizens. During the mid-nineteenth century the town had about 200 residents who tended—with some notable exceptions—to be pro-Southern. While some county residents volunteered to fight to preserve the Union or waited to be called up by the draft, a far larger contingent "went South" to fight for Southern independence.

The day after Virginia left the Union, the first blood of the war was drawn in Baltimore when pro-Southern mobs attacked units of Pennsylvania and Massachusetts volunteers marching through the city on their way to Washington. For the next four days, Baltimore was torn by riots in which four Northern soldiers and 36 Marylanders were killed. This event inspired the state song "Maryland, My Maryland," a call to support the South.

It did not take long for the Federal government to realize that Maryland would have to be kept in the Union by force of arms. Before the month was over Federal armies occupied much of the state, pro-Southern newspapers (including the county's leading journal, the Montgomery County *Sentinel*) were suppressed, the writ of habeus corpus was suspended, and pro-Southern legislators were imprisoned. Brute force guaranteed that Maryland would not secede.

In June 1861, Colonel Charles P. Stone led a Union army of occupation into Montgomery County. The Rockville Expedition moved west along Rockville Pike, then along Darnestown Road to Poolesville and Point of Rocks. Large detachments were left at Seneca and Darnestown, at Clopper's, and at Muddy Branch.

In 1861, the Muddy Branch area consisted of a tiny settlement at Quince Orchard, some small farms, and a few huge plantations such as those owned by slaveholders John DuFief (present-day North Potomac) and Frederick Tschiffely (now the site of Kentlands, Washingtonian Woods, and National Geographic/Lakelands). Skirmishes and small engagements were fought throughout the war in the Poolesville, Clopper's, Darnestown, and Muddy Branch areas.

For most of the war Gaithersburg served as a transit point for a steady stream of Union forces and supplies. Occasionally the stream grew stronger, and in September 1862, it became a torrent as the center of General George McClellan's army moved through Gaithersburg and his left wing marched through Muddy Branch and Darnestown on their way to fight at South Mountain and Antietam.

From time to time the stream reversed, as when detachments of Confederate colonel John Singleton Mosby's Partisan Rangers, the units of the 35th Virginia led by Captain George S. Chiswell (Chiswell's Exile Band), or Colonel Elijah "Lige" Veirs White (the Commanches) raided the many Union camps along Darnestown Road.

On June 27, 1863, Confederate general J.E.B. Stuart led his cavalry across the Potomac River at Rowser's Ford. He split his command and one brigade, under General Wade Hampton, rode to Darnestown, then down Darnestown Road through Muddy Branch to Rockville. There they met brigades led by General Fitzhugh Lee and General W.H.F. (Rooney) Lee (under Colonel John R. Chambliss) and captured a huge Union supply train of 125 wagons and 700 mules. Union losses in that engagement numbered more than 400. Stuart's men spent an idyllic afternoon flirting with the women at the Rockville

This view of a Civil War reenactment at Monocacy was captured on film by Gaithersburg resident Bob Johnson.

Female Academy and passing time with the citizens of the town, which was, as one Northerner wrote, "a vile Secesh hole."

Perhaps because supplies were at a premium in the South, Stuart decided to take the supply train with him rather than destroy it. The wagons and the prisoners slowed the normally swift progress of Stuart's cavalry. The prisoners were paroled in small groups as Stuart moved through Maryland, but he refused to abandon the supplies. In consequence Stuart did not arrive in Gettysburg until the third day of the battle, long after it had taken a decisive turn in favor of the North.

Confederate general Robert E. Lee, who relied on Stuart's cavalry for reconnaissance and information, called them his "eyes and ears." Some historians believe Stuart's dillydallying in Rockville and his late arrival in Gettysburg were the critical factors in the Union victory at that battle. They argue that the Civil War was really lost with Stuart's dalliance in Montgomery County.

In July 1864, the last great Confederate offensive of the Civil War passed through Gaithersburg and Muddy Branch. Confederate general Jubal Early led a corps of the Army of Northern Virginia through the Shenandoah Valley into Maryland, and on July 9 captured Frederick City. At mid-day, the citizens of Frederick paid a ransom of $200,000 in gold to the Southerners. That afternoon, Early's corps met and defeated a Union army led by General Lew Wallace, later famous as the author of the epic novel *Ben Hur*, in a bloody battle at Monocacy near what is now Francis Scott Key Mall in Frederick. As the battle ended, Early set his sights on Washington, D.C.

On July 10, the advance guards of Early's corps under General John McCausland engaged the U.S. 16th Pennsylvania under Major William Fry near present-day Derwood. Fry's units fell back into Rockville and held their ground for a time in spirited fighting in the center of town, then fell back once again and re-formed on a hill south of town where Richard Montgomery High School now stands. After an artillery barrage, Fry gave way and McCausland chased the broken force into Bethesda before returning to Rockville.

That night the main body of Early's corps camped at Summit Hall on the former site of Logtown owned by John T. DeSellum, a slaveowner who was nonetheless a prominent Union sympathizer. DeSellum, who headed the U.S. Draft Board for Montgomery County, had been captured in Rockville the year before during Stuart's raid and had been paroled in Brookeville. Like most pro-Union parolees, DeSellum ignored the conditions of his parole after his release and continued to work actively for the Northern cause.

DeSellum's reputation as a Unionist slaveholder was well known. While the officers chatted amiably with their host at dinner, the farm was ransacked and plundered. Chickens and livestock were carried off, horses were commandeered, and DeSellum was given a promissory note and two barrels of corn. He was not left destitute, however, because his quick-thinking sister Sarah had concealed some $3,000 in gold by sewing it into her underskirt. She knew Southern honor meant that she would not be subjected to an embarrassing personal search. The hidden gold was not found.

On July 11 and 12, a series of battles took place in Montgomery County and the District of Columbia. At Muddy Branch, Confederate colonel Mosby's rangers raided the camp of the 8th Illinois Cavalry, capturing horses and supplies before setting the camp on fire. At Clopper's, 21-year-old William D. Scott of the 14th Virginia was wounded while foraging

This is another scene from a Civil War reenactment at Monocacy that was photographed by Gaithersburg resident Bob Johnson.

on the farm of John Taney. Scott fled to nearby "Woodlands," the Clopper family home, where he died. He was buried in secret that night by the pro-Southern Clopper family in the graveyard at St. Rose of Lima Catholic Church. A small area of Civil War graves exists today in the churchyard.

Early's failed assault on Washington and its aftermath constituted the last major troop movements in the area, although intermittent raids and skirmishes continued. The last Confederate raid on the county took place at Edward's Ferry on February 25, 1865. Montgomery County continued to be occupied territory until the end of the war. When the Lincoln assassination conspirator George Atzerodt attempted his escape along a route through Gaithersburg and upper Montgomery County, he was captured by Union troops soon after reaching Germantown.

For Montgomery County, the Northern victory meant preservation of the Union and freedom for several thousand slaves. The county continued to be a sleepy Southern agricultural community until well into the twentieth century however, and the last vestiges of the war and Reconstruction did not disappear until the 1970s.

The most potent remaining symbols of the Civil War are the Confederate graves in cemeteries scattered throughout the county, a Confederate memorial chapel in Beallsville, and a monument in Rockville dedicated in 1912 to the "heroes" of Montgomery County's "thin grey line." Atop the monument, which stands in the shadow of the Old Red Brick Court House, is a statue of a Confederate soldier. The old warrior faces toward the South, as if still contemplating the "Lost Cause."

5. SOCIAL LIFE

In the nineteenth century, Gaithersburg was proud of the intellectual accomplishments of its citizens. It aspired to be the social center of the county if not the legal center as the new county seat. These ambitions were accompanied by a strong moral and social idealism common to the period and resulted in the founding of temperance groups, literary societies, fraternal organizations, agricultural organizations, and other purely social interest groups. Their role was to provide professional exchanges, continuing education, musical and dramatic entertainment, and dinner out of the home with pleasant company. In short, they represented the extras in life that are often provided today by commercial entertainment and restaurants.

THE GRANGE

Gaithersburg was established as an agricultural town and had an agricultural society, the Patrons of Husbandry, Grange no. 53. The Grange in Gaithersburg was organized March 14, 1874 by Granger Deputy Colonel Washington Bowie of the Olney area. John T. DeSellum was the first master and probably the chief supporter of the group. James B. Gaither was the overseer, and Robert Briggs, John E. Thompson, W.R. Fulks, James H. Clagett, Richard Mills, Issac Ranney, Joseph Thompson, and others of their families also served. The group seemed to be off to a fine start. In 1876, the planned construction of a Grange Hall and store was heralded by an anonymous *Sentinel* correspondent as "one of the greatest benefits to both Grange and town," adding, "Gaithersburg is and will be the same place of forty years ago unless some such steps of improvement are taken." The hall was the second story of the Gaithersburg School.

However, the Grange was not mentioned in a pamphlet published about the town in 1891 after a fire destroyed the school and Grange Hall. It was removed from the tax rolls of the city on March 24, 1896, but the fire was probably not the only reason for the group's demise. The Catholic Church had ruled the Grange to be a secret society and therefore forbidden to all good Catholics. None of the founding Grange officers were Catholic, but some of the town's leading citizens and farmers were, including the Diamond, Gloyd, and Clements families. The death of John DeSellum in 1891 probably undermined the group further, but finally it becomes obvious that Gaithersburg was not so much a farming community as the commercial and transportation hub of an agricultural area. Its citizens formed cultural and social groups around many interests. Gaithersburg's social scene included people such as Francis Cassat Clopper, the uncle of artist Mary Cassatt, and his son-in-law W.R. Hutton, a world famous civil engineer. Needless to say, the social organizations of the period had remarkable standards and ambition, and perhaps even more remarkable accomplishments.

Lee Lipscomb, in his 1891 pamphlet extolling the virtues of the town to prospective new residents, said, "A stranger can not help being impressed with the air of refinement and good breeding that characterizes the inhabitants of Gaithersburg. Their numerous intellectual and social organizations give unmistakable evidence of culture." By 1890, the town had absorbed the efforts of a number of earlier cultural societies and had established a receptive climate for the well-regarded Waverly and Jefferson Literary Clubs. This was the village's real period of social glory.

In 1890, Gaithersburg campaigned to get the new courthouse and thus become the county seat because of its central location. It sparked a rivalry with Rockville that extended to all endeavors, social ones included. Facilities for large gatherings were built and used, including Diamond Hall in 1878, Summit Hotel in 1881, and later a veritable host of other halls.

These social events typically had some entertainment or dancing until supper was served around midnight. Dancing continued, usually to a band imported from Washington, until 5:00 a.m. Guests reportedly came from as far away as Philadelphia, Baltimore, Georgetown, and Washington as well as the local area. The sumptuous gowns, the names, and the best features of the beauties were recounted at length.

The 1895 Summit Hotel was the scene of many early social events.

EARLY SOCIAL AND CULTURAL GROUPS

The Montgomery Amateur Drama Club (MADC) was Gaithersburg's earliest known cultural group. Some of the tickets and scripts from its "entertainments" are preserved in the Woodlands Collection of the Montgomery County Historical Society, part of the collected papers and memorabilia of W.R. Hutton.

The Huttons were not residents of Gaithersburg, although they owned property within the town limits, but they made great contributions to the town. Hutton was a famous engineer and world traveler with a taste for the arts. His papers contain programs from ballet, musical performances, and theater. They also contain the scripts of 26 plays and sketches of which only *David Garrick* is known to have been produced by the MADC.

On December 16, 1878, the group presented two pieces, *Meg's Diversion*, and *The Two Puddifoots*, followed by an oyster supper. The *Sentinel* also commented that "The Membership of the M.A.D.C. comprises the beauty, elegance and culture of the vicinity of Gaithersburg and previous entertainments have won for the club a reputation for considerable amateur historic talent." The club was composed of some of the oldest area families: the Diamond, Meem, Clopper, Farrel, Maddox, and Hutton families. Of one production, the *Sentinel* reviewer mentioned the "professional rate quality" but another time commented that more attention could be paid to memorizing the lines and to the curtain. On several occasions, the troupe "toured" after its run in Gaithersburg, visiting Barnesville and Rockville. The club is documented as active from 1877 to 1879 but the number of unmentioned scripts in the Woodlands Collection suggests that its life may have been longer.

Another cultural group, the Gaithersburg Literary and Singing Society, was also active in 1879. This organization gave an entertainment of musical solos and quartets followed by a buffet on Saturday afternoon, August 1, of that year, under the direction of John E. Clagett.

Even the baseball team joined the cultural parade, if minstrel shows can be termed cultural. The Darnestown Base Ball Club (the Darnestown election district included a portion of Gaithersburg) gave a minstrel show at Diamond Hall on February 11, 1879 and another on February 18. Their efforts must have been well received by the public as the show was later presented at Mechanicsville (Olney) Grange Hall. This team reorganized in July 1879 as the Forest Oak Base Ball Club and prepared another show for December 18, 1879, "the whole . . . to be strictly moral." Proceeds were to "add to the fund for the purchase of the monument to the Confederate dead" near Urbana, a frequent recipient of Gaithersburg donations.

Another group, the Woodside Musical Club, was founded in March 1880. Its members "constitute a full string band with all the attendant prerequisites . . . object, social enjoyment and mutual improvement." The club leased Diamond Hall for its home and announced that it would rent to others. The *Sentinel* of July 9, 1880 advertised that the group was to give a performance of music and dancing at Diamond Hall on Tuesday evening, July 22, "for the benefit of an Episcopal Church to be raised." The very next week, on the 27th, the club was to give a performance of "Ethiopian Sketches, Dutch and Irish Impersonations, [and] Plantation Melodies."

This ticket was for an 1877 performance by the MADC.

In 1881, the club attracted the attention of its neighbors in Rockville, according to this report in the *Sentinel*:

> On Tuesday night last a complimentary hop was given at Diamond Hall, Gaithersburg, by the Woodside Musical Club. It was another of those occasions on which the people of that town, as they always do, so generously dispensed their hospitality and made their town more popular with their guests, who feel a deep gratitude for the pleasure afforded them. It was largely attended by handsome ladies finely dressed and gentlemen from all parts of the county and a distance, who participated in the all-night dance to the music of Coles band of Washington, and partook of a sumptuous supper that was given.

Interest in literary and musical groups remained high in the town. A notice appeared in the *Sentinel* of December 28, 1888 announcing that "The young ladies and gentlemen of Gaithersburg will give a musical and literary entertainment in the Grange Hall on the 31st. The proceeds will be applied to the purchase of instruments for the brass band of the burg."

Another anonymous correspondent "Spectator" described the event for the *Sentinel* and reported the Grange Hall, with a seating capacity of 200, "filled to the utmost capacity." Miss Kate Walek on organ; George W. Meem, violin; and Mr. Willard on flute evidently gave an excellent performance. "It is not often our pleasure to listen to such music," commented Spectator, who wished the Central Brass Band "unlimited success and a grand future."

TABLEAUX VIVANTS

AT

DIAMOND HALL,

GAITHERSBURG, MD.,

On WEDNESDAY, 1st of June, 1881.

1. PINAFORE.

2. VIRGINIUS.

3. TRIAL OF CAPT. JOHN SMITH.

4. BAPTISM OF POCAHONTAS.

5. SLAVE MARKET IN BAGDAD.

This program is from an 1881 Gaithersburg production. (Courtesy of Montgomery County Historical Society.)

This group was still active in 1890 and planning "a dramatic literary entertainment" to be given at Norman Hall on February 19. It was to go to Olney after this. The Central Brass Band was active almost to the end of the century, although perhaps not continuously. It officially reorganized in 1897 with Harvey Gladhill, mayor at the time, elected president and W. Clarence Duvall, Frank Ricketts, and Perry Gloyd filling other offices. The format of the club was unchanged. A planned future program was entitled *A Country Band*, including the farce *Box and Cox*. William H. Wessels was in charge of preparations and Professor T.M. Turner was the director.

Professor Turner also led another local group, Turner's Cornet Band. The general nature of this band was the same as the Brass Band. On February 4, 1898, the comedy *A Married Bachelor* was to be given by "an experienced cast . . . under the direction of Mr. Jack Carlton, the popular young author and comedian" at Norman Hall. The proceeds were to go to the Cornet Band.

It was obvious that Gaithersburg had a taste for music. This brought the town some notoriety of a unique kind in 1890. An advertisement in the *Sentinel* for Miller Organs entitled "Gaithersburg Ahead" begins, "Probably no place in the State of its size has demonstrated its taste for music of late so much as Gaithersburg and vicinity."

One of the buyers who gave testimony for the organ in the ad was Reverend J.L. Lodge of the Baptist Church. The Reverend Dr. Lodge was one of the fundamental spirits behind the exceptionally high ethical and intellectual idealism that prevailed during the 1880s and 1890s. Lodge's influence is even more impressive considering that there was no Baptist congregation in the town. He was greatly aided by E.L. Amiss, the town's schoolmaster and an active member of Forest Oak Methodist Episcopal Church South.

By 1884, the MADC and Woodside Musical Club seemed to be inactive. The last known event was a "select" (by invitation only) Mask Ball, held at Diamond Hall on Monday, February 28, 1881. The select danced to a Washington band, admired each other's costumes, ate a midnight supper, and kept dancing until dawn. Mrs. Diamond naturally appeared as the Queen of Diamonds.

In August 1881, the Summit Hotel social season opened under the management of Juan Boyle. After this, Boyle's catered affairs diminished the need for local committees and clubs to organize such functions except for private occasions. Boyle's soirees were elaborate events that attracted an occasional senator and other distinguished guests to the town. John Diamond was one of the leaders in the corporation of local businessmen who financed, built, and leased the hotel.

TEMPERANCE CLUBS

Temperance was another issue that inspired active organizations. John DeSellum was a member of the Middlebrook Temperance Club, the oldest in the county, and the Methodist Church started a Women's Christian Temperance Union (WCTU). In addition to the destruction of liquor traffic, total abstinence, and the reform of drunkards, the WCTU advocated progressive social changes: a living wage for all workers, an eight-hour work day, equal civil rights for both sexes, and a single moral standard. The group followed the teachings of Frances Willard. Grace Methodist Episcopal Church South held a Frances E. Willard memorial service on Sunday, February 25, 1917.

> A special program has been arranged, so good speakers and good music may be
> expected. Everybody is cordially invited to come and spend a profitable evening.
> Every white ribboner is earnestly requested to be present. Don't forget to wear
> your white ribbon bow and kindly take seat in the front pews and let it be seen
> that you are out and out for the temperance cause.

A white ribbon indicated a faithful lifetime pledge to complete abstinence, red ribbons and blue ribbons were worn by reformed drinkers. Gaithersburg Good Templars Lodge no. 217 was another Methodist-supported temperance group. The Good Templars were active from 1884 until 1898.

With the intense temperance fervor of the time and the residue of Civil War animosity, it was inevitable that conflict would arise. Both the Good Templars and the later Waverly Literary Club experienced division in 1894–1895, with Reverend James L. Lodge, E.L. Amiss, Thomas English, and others of uncompromisingly high intellectual standards on one side, and those who felt participation, variety, and a little innocent amusement could also be virtues of a public organization on the other side.

A common social outing was attending a school play such as this 1933 production of Nothing but the Truth *at the high school.*

The Independent Order of Good Templars (IOGT) was the older of the two to experience division. As with other long-lived groups, it had a leader devoted to its success over the years. As DeSellum was the mainstay of the Grangers, so E.L. Amiss was to the Good Templars. Ironically, Amiss attended to its birth as an officer, nursed it along in its first years, tended the cradle during its lifetime and saw it grow, and then was directed to deliver its death blow in 1898.

The group had a strong beginning. In March 1884, its second month, IOGT reported 32 members. In 1885, with "about 60 members," the lodge put on the temperance play *Ten Nights in a Bar Room* to raise money for an organ. It acquired a hall, the location of which is now unknown, and was present at many civic events. It established an order of Juvenile Templars who mixed their abstinence lessons with ice cream and picnics. The group was unusual because it, like the Grange, accepted both men and women for membership.

Each member had to complete three degrees before becoming a full member: "Heart," which taught self-duty and the necessity of complete abstinence; "Charity," which taught duty to others; and "Royal Virtue," which taught duty to God. The admission of women led to ribald rumors among the opposition that the group was actually a free-love society.

Such rumors did not end Gaithersburg Lodge no. 217. It remained strong until 1895, when a second lodge, La Gascogne Lodge no. 306, IOGT was formed. Unfortunately, this resulted in two weaker and highly competitive groups. When the La Gascogne Lodge announced its second anniversary celebration for Friday night, February 19th, 1897 at 7:30 p.m., with an open invitation for the public to attend the "very interesting program," the older group seemingly pulled out all the stops.

The *Sentinel* of February 19, 1897 advertised an entertainment that very evening at the "Town Hall." Among the promised attractions were "vocals and instrument music by Prof. W.H. Dunawin, the famous banjoist of the south; vocal music by the Anti-Tweat Quartet; short address by Capt. James S.B. Hartsock of Washington; temperance tableau by local talent in charge of Prof. Vernon Watkins." Needless to say, the Gaithersburg Lodge no. 217, "one of the oldest and strongest in the State," celebrated its 13th anniversary with a "large audience."

The rivalry was fired up, not dampened, by such competition, and it is significant that at the 1897 annual meeting of the district lodge no. 1, IOGT, composed of 13 subordinate lodges in the county, the only chapters singled out in the newspaper account were the two rivals: Gaithersburg and La Gascogne Lodges.

The district meeting of 1898 was entertained by La Gascogne Lodge. E.L. Amiss was re-elected District Chief Templar. At this meeting, "the differences existing between the Good Templar Lodges of Gaithersburg received the attention of the session, and having obtained their acquiescence in the matter the District Lodge decided to memorialize the Grand Lodge to revoke the charters of these lodges, with the understanding that they would reorganize into one strong lodge. Evidently the reorganization did not occur, as this was the last mention of any Gaithersburg Good Templar Lodge to be found.

THE WAVERLY AND JEFFERSON LITERARY CLUBS

The same fate was to befall the most famous of all Gaithersburg's early organizations, the Waverly Club. The club was organized March 12, 1889, "by six gentlemen." The first president was Reverend J.L. Lodge, D.D. Our first knowledge of it comes from the publication in the *Sentinel* on April 26, 1889, of an essay by Dr. Lodge entitled "Some Elements of True Courage," taken from the club journal *The Waverly Progress*. A letter to the *Sentinel* dated May 27, 1889 gives us an idea of the membership, purposes, and structure of the club:

> The club was called to order by its respected and much-loved President, Dr. Lodge, who presided with dignity and ease. Too much can not be said of the worthy gentleman who has labored so earnestly and diligently for the success of the Waverly and its motive, a library, for the use and benefit of the young of the village. And just here, let me add, that his endeavors have been crowned with success, for the Waverly Club now own one hundred and ten choice volumes by distinguished authors.
>
> After the secretary Mr. Sterick called the roll, the club proceeded with its program: reading of essays and pieces by the president and other members, which included pieces by "our gray-haired townsman, Mr. J.T. DeSellum, who never fails to instruct," an original piece by Mrs. Helen Hogan entitled "What Can'st Be?" full of spicy jokes on the members, a selection from Emerson and several other pieces. After this the audience was entertained by Mrs. Hogan who read "Over the Hill to the Poor House," followed by a speech by T.I. Owen, who spoke on "The Depravity of the Present Generation." Mr. Heltzell read a

An 1896 social event at the Belt Building drew townspeople together.

beautiful selection entitled "Rain Drops," after which the wit of the Club, Mr. Merriwether, declaimed "Man's Wants" in such an excellent manner that it brought tears to many eyes from excessive laughter, after which he read "Parody on Woman's Wants," amid shouts of applause.

In January 1890, the club found a home in John A. Belt's "commodious and elegant hall." Waverly's first anniversary meeting at Norman Hall on March 12, 1890 was attended "by the largest audience we have ever had probably 150 persons. All feel that trial time is passed and that the sun now shines for Waverly."

Lodge's anniversary essay told of the efforts to establish the club: "We began with out a book, or a penny's worth of property; today our library numbers 327 books; and the entire property of the Club is worth $300. The membership numbers 51 and steadily increases."

But in 1894 the *Sentinel* notes, "We regret to learn that the Rev. J.L. Lodge and his accomplished daughter, Miss Lillian, have withdrawn from the 'Waverly Club,' of Gaithersburg. The Doctor stood at the cradle of this club, and we had indulged the hope that he would have continued to give it the influence of his scholarly attainments, energy and experience for many years to come."

The Waverly continued without Lodge. At the June 1894 meeting, an all-male panel debated the question of women's suffrage. On June 29, the club proclaimed its incorporation and intent to build a hall and reading room.

The society did not seem to falter. In fact, in January 1897, it announced the election of its new officers and proudly stated: "The library of the organization is one of the best in the State." However, this tranquil period was soon to end when the club encountered active competition from its old mentor, Lodge. The cause of the rift between Dr. Lodge and the club remained a mystery until 1898 when the Jefferson Club published its first notice in the *Sentinel* on February 25, 1898. The aim of the new group was obvious: to restore it to its former high intellectual level. This is made abundantly clear at the end of the message:

> In accordance with a sentiment which has been gaining strength for the past five years, a body of citizens of Gaithersburg and vicinity assembled in Forest Oak Hall, February 3rd, 1898, for the purpose of organizing a literary club, its object, the cultivation of its members through literary exercises, and the founding of a library for the exclusive use of its own members. At an adjourned meeting, held February 19th, officers were elected as follows: President, Dr. James L. Lodge; Vice-President, E.L. Amiss; Secretary, Carson Ward; Treasurer, D.B. Carlisle; Sergeant-At-Arms, James T. English.
>
> The club starts with a membership of twenty-six. Applications for membership are steadily coming in. With its scholarly and eminent president, whose unremitting, disinterested labors, and large personal gifts of money, in four years brought an organization, which had a like design, to such a height of distinction that its fame extended far beyond the borders of the State, of which distinguished non-residents were proud to be honorary members, and leaving it at the end of that period with a splendid library of over 1,000 books. The people believe the club will eventually become an efficient and influential body. A polite and appreciative public will be welcome, provided it expects to be instructed. Any looking for entertainment must look for it elsewhere.

The new club had an effect on the Waverly even before the official announcement. In January 1898, the Waverly voted to admit the general public to its entertainments. Meetings were planned for the second and fourth Tuesdays of each month and the librarians would furnish books to patrons "at their pleasure." At the February 8 meeting, instrumental solos and recitations by the pupils at Dr. Water's Fairview School constituted the program. The club invited young ladies to join the group free of charge, and six applications were submitted. Almost as in answer to the forthcoming charges, the Waverly stated, "The club is progressive and bids fair to reach that goal to which it started and for which it has so faithfully labored."

In March, after the Jefferson Club had been formally introduced, the Waverly voted to admit any 16-year-old student at any school in Gaithersburg free of charge. In May, the club ladies announced an entertainment and musical at the Opera House to benefit the club.

Dr. Lodge, Amiss, DeSellum, English, and the others appear to have been focused on forming the private equivalent of a college-level seminar group. The early programs show that each member was asked to submit the best of his/her specialty so that the others could share in this knowledge. There were musical interludes, but the thrust of the program was for quality literary material, either by famous authors or by the members themselves. This level of excellence could not be maintained with members of weaker literary backgrounds. The presentations would have to be brought down to the level of all.

The Waverly had become something quite different. Not better or worse necessarily, but different. The best solution, viewed with hindsight, would have been to allow each club to fill its need and let the town benefit. But it did not happen that way. The two were committed to the same goals (written, in fact, by the same man) and each was determined to prove its method best.

Thus, like the Good Templars, they entered into a competition. For a while the town basked in fine entertainments like "oxy-hydrogen light views . . . over 100 beautifully colored views . . . unsurpassed by anything shown in large cities," and prominent speakers. Inevitably however, both weakened and died.

Apparently the Waverly Club was the first to go. Laura Conlon, the daughter of William H. Wessells, who had been active in the Waverly and probably also in the Jefferson, recalls that the library was first located above Belt's store (where the Waverly met) and then at Carson Ward's store (where the Jefferson met). However it happened, the Waverly was dead by 1900 and its books became the property of its rival. The Jefferson considered disbanding in 1902, but reconsidered. It was still active in 1904 but holding only annual meetings. On October 9, 1905, the Jefferson donated its library of more than 1,000 books and $15 to the public school. The town was not to have another public library until the 1930s when the Gaithersburg Homemakers Club made the founding of a public library its chief objective.

BASEBALL AND ATHLETIC CLUBS

The stress and tension of 1894 probably contributed to Gaithersburg's one truly comic episode: The Great Baseball Escapade. Through the years, the town has had a love-hate relationship with baseball. Most of the time it has been love, but in 1894, the sport was declared illegal twice and two leading citizens, Dr. J.H. McCormick (the town druggist and a prominent Mason) and ex-sheriff and telephone company employee Frank Farrell were sent to jail for playing the game. The history of Gaithersburg baseball up until that time is far less exciting.

The first team known in Gaithersburg was the Modoc Club of 1873. It was evidently named for the Modoc Indian tribe in Oregon, which received extensive coverage in the *Sentinel* through the summer of 1873. The Modocs massacred U.S. troops on several occasions and survived untouched due to their "natural fastness" until they finally were captured and massacred in turn. No game scores were reported in the 1873 newspapers, so it is not known whether the team justified its name through natural fastness or by being massacred.

The Modocs were succeeded by the Darnestown Base Ball Club. This club played a schedule of opposing town's teams including some from Washington. In 1879, it reorganized as the Forest Oak Base Ball Club, formerly the Darnestown Base Ball Club. It held its meetings near the B&O Railroad station.

The arrest and imprisonment incident in 1894 was the result of an alleged violation of a Gaithersburg town ordinance concerning disturbing the peace. The original ordinance is lost, but the revised version of 1894, ordinance no. 9, lumps baseball in with such

Visiting athletic clubs often stayed at the Forest Oak Hotel.

prohibited offenses as wild driving, bean shooting, public drunkenness, profanity, firecrackers, and using creedmores (small target rifles) and crossbows in the streets. Violators were subject to arrest and a fine plus the bailiff's fee.

The classification of such seemingly harmless pastimes as bean shooting and baseball with such generally unacceptable habits as drunkenness and wild driving was probably out of concern for safety. A well-hit ball could easily damage property or unsuspecting individuals, or even frighten horses, and a runaway horse could be lethal. Another reason may have been the high ethical standards that prevailed in the town. The Methodist Church did not prohibit baseball itself, but the games seemed to attract other "worldly amusements" and pastimes that were considered detrimental such as gambling, drinking, and profanity. Baseball itself had been declared illegal on Sundays in an earlier court case, as it was thought to desecrate the Sabbath.

The first report of the arrest and imprisonment of the two men reached the county through the pages of the *Sentinel*:

> On Friday of last week A.F. Fairall and Dr. John H. McCormick, of
> Gaithersburg, were arrested by the bailiff of Gaithersburg and taken before
> Charles F. Duvall, President of the Commissioners, on the charge of an alleged
> violation of a corporation ordinance in regard to playing baseball. They were
> tried, found guilty, and a fine of $1 and costs was imposed upon each. In default
> of payment of the fine they were committed to jail. They were released from jail

the same evening by Judge John T. Vinson on a writ of habeus corpus. Mr. Fairall and Dr. McCormick contend that the whole proceedings were irregular and void, and have instructed their counsel, Mr. Robert B. Peter, to enter suit for $5,000 damages for false imprisonment.

The town minutes add some details to this account. At the meeting of the Gaithersburg Board of Commissioners on June 20, 1894, the bailiff reported that the arrests had been made "for Ball playing on lot owned by T.B. Brooks."

President C.D. "Frank" Duvall stated that the above parties were brought before him and that he had fined them $1.85 each for committing said nuisance in default of which they were committed to the county jail. The clerk read a letter from R.B. Peters of Rockville stating that he was about to enter suit against the commissioners and the bailiff in the sum of $5,000 each for false arrest and imprisonment and that he would be pleased to consider any offer they may make pending a settlement.

The commissioners were unmoved by the threatened suit. After the corporation attorney defined the law, Commissioner Lee Lipscomb moved to approve the actions of the president and bailiff. They then adopted an even stronger and more specific ordinance against baseball, which stated that "No game of baseball shall be allowed to be played within the corporate limits at any time without the consent of the commissioners."

Twenty-five copies of the new ordinance were printed and posted. The lawsuit is not reported in subsequent minutes, so it presumably was dropped. At the next meeting of

The Gaithersburg Athletic Club baseball team posed for this photograph in 1910.

June 29, 1894, Commissioner Lee Lipscomb asked permission to play ball on lots owned by him on behalf of several young men and received it "until objections be made by the immediate neighbors."

However, in July, Mrs. Thompson and Mr. and Mrs. Spates wrote to the commission to complain of ball-playing in front of their residences. Finally, the Ideal Base Ball Club, petitioning through Lipscomb, received permission to play on the lot owned by Miss Blanche M. Spates. Ironically, the final location for this "sinful" sport was a 4- or 5-acre clearing in a wooded tract behind the present City Hall called "Paradise."

This was the final chorus, but not the last note. There must have been some residual dissatisfaction with the whole business because in 1895 the council passed ordinance no. 18, which prohibited the tearing down, removal, or mutilation of posted ordinances.

Baseball regained its former respectability by 1900, and the town teams played local and visiting teams. A page from the old Forest Oak Hotel register tells us of one of the more colorful traveling teams. The club registered as "GRRns Nebraska Indians," a play on the name of the manager Guy W. Green of Lincoln, Nebraska. Green, Tabashekeshiek, Shane, Miguel, Young Deer, Wolf, Twin, and the others billed themselves as "the greatest team of genuine Indians in the World . . . the Nebraska Indian Base Ball Team." If not the greatest, they were at least better than the Gaithersburg locals since the scores written in the register favor the Indians 8-5 and 6-2.

The baseball field was later moved to the corner of Montgomery and Frederick Avenues. In 1910, the Gaithersburg Athletic Club was formed. This group promoted many sports, not just baseball. Some, like basketball, were so new that few local competitors could be found to challenge. According to Claude Owen, one of the most memorable town teams was fielded during the Athletic Club period. It featured three sons of John Diamond: John Bernard Jr., Herbert, and Douglas Diamond. All three were close in age and had played on the Georgetown University baseball team. They "added a lot of weight," in Owen's words.

In 1922, a group known as the Gaithersburg Athletic Association was incorporated. A similar group, the Gaithersburg Sports Association, is active today and organizes a variety of sports leagues for different age groups. Youth athletic activities are not new to the city. In 1879, an archery club composed of "young ladies and gentlemen of Gaithersburg" was formed, and Claude Owen also mentions that track and field events were held every summer around where the junior high school is now located. There were foot races, high jumping, pole vaulting, bicycle races, and on several occasions a jousting tournament was held with the jouster mounted on horseback trying to impale a suspended ring.

In addition to these activities, outdoor sports such as hunting, fishing, and shooting were common pastimes and often helped put food on the table. Gaithersburg had one of the first early conservation groups, a Sportsmen Organization dedicated to the protection of game, to rigid enforcement of the game laws, and to the passage of other laws for the preservation of the game that survived the hunting season. Although this early club cannot be traced beyond its initial mention, Gaithersburg citizens have demonstrated a constant interest in conservation and outdoor sports. Many resident sportsmen have been active in the Isaac Walton League, which has its National Conservation Park in Gaithersburg near the National Institute of Standards and Technology on Muddy Branch Road.

POLITICAL ORGANIZATIONS

Another interest was politics. Both Republican and Democratic clubs existed on the county level and had members from Gaithersburg, but organizations limited to the local area were generally campaign clubs formed to support a specific slate of candidates. There were many of these, including the Greeley and Brown Clubs of Forest Oak, and the later Hancock and English Clubs.

The Hancock Club held a Democratic rally in Gaithersburg at which the president T.J. Owen made a speech, and Juan Boyle introduced the next speaker, Montgomery Blair. Following Blair's remarks, the crowd retired to Mr. Boyle's residence for refreshments and entertainment. These rallies often featured the raising of a pole: a flagpole displaying a banner manufactured by a loyal party seamstress and which prominently displayed the candidates' names.

Gaithersburg was somewhat unusual in the 1870s in that it had both Republican and Democrat supporters. Republicans were considered Northern sympathizers and the county was largely Southern in allegiance.

In 1879, John T. DeSellum, secretary of the Republican club, announced a meeting to be held at Gaithersburg in August that was later reported in the strongly Democratic *Sentinel* on September 19, 1879 under the title "Queer Methods:"

The Forest Oak Lodge no. 123 of the Knights of Pythias built its new Castle Hall in 1911.

The mongrel meeting at Gaithersburg and the Republican convention suggest no little novelty in political plotting and no little dirtiness in their attempt to hoodwink the people novel because the people are presumed to be fools; dirty because they promise what is impossible. One fact is evident the tax-payers' convention did not "tumble" to those pretty resolutions passed at Diamond Hall. Hence it is that the destiny of the Radical party is entrusted to Arthur Stabler, Frank Mace, Frank Bell, Wm. I. Cook, and one or two more of that way of thinking.

These gentlemen are partisans, malignant in Radical dye. . . . They will look only to stealing a foot-hold for their despised and despicable party.

Democrats remained strong in the county and in the town but little is said of the progress of the Republicans in the local newspapers. In 1898, a Lincoln Republican Club was active, but its connection with the earlier organization is not known.

Considering these few remnants of Civil War bitterness in the town, it is comforting to discover that the 1890s produced some organizations of lasting good. While the Good Templars and the Literary Clubs were dividing and falling, two fraternal lodges were founded that are still flourishing. The Knights of Pythias, Forest Oak Lodge no. 123; and the Pentalpha Lodge no. 194, Ancient and Accepted Free Masons were formed, respectively, in 1892 and 1893.

THE KNIGHTS OF PYTHIAS

The Forest Oak Lodge of the Knights of Pythias drew heavily on the Forest Oak Church for its members. The Jefferson Club did likewise and the Knights' officer list for 1897 reads like a carbon copy of the Jefferson's: E.L. Amiss, James T. English, John T. Martin, David Carlisle, Albert Phebus, George Selby, Carson Ward, E.H. Etchison, and David F. Virts. In fact, both groups had their halls over Carson Ward's store on the northeast corner of Brooks and Frederick Avenues.

Since Professor Amiss was a charter member of the group, it should come as no surprise that the lodge, which holds to the principles of friendship, charity, and benevolence, also endorsed temperance in its first years. On February 22, 1894, the Knights produced *Ten Nights in a Bar Room* at Norman Hall. In March, the production went on tour to Poolesville and Clarksburg. The lodge was active in civic life and appeared as a body at many ceremonial events, dedications, and holiday celebrations.

MASONIC ORDERS

The Knights was closely followed by the Pentalpha Lodge of Masons, which received its charter on November 22, 1893. The first officers were Robert M. Moore, E.D. Kingsley, John A. Belt, P.M. Smith, and N.B. Cramer. Reverend Moore was the pastor of Epworth Methodist Episcopal Church at the time.

The group first met over Nicholl's Harness Shop on Diamond Avenue in Diamond Hall, which had resounded with music and dancing feet a few years before. In 1898, the

Masonic Hall was struck by lightning. Besides considerable damage to the building, the Scottish Rite sustained losses amounting to $400. The loss of property and housing may have prompted the group to build their own hall at 8 Russell Avenue in 1899. This hall, like the Pythian Hall, was a principal meeting place and the first moving picture house for the community before it was torn down in 1976. In addition to the Perfection Lodge, there was an order of Knights Templar, a York Rite body of Masons. Montgomery Commandery no. 13 was the first commandery of Knights Templar in the county. It was formed with customary Masonic pomp and ritual in April 1902.

The Masons played an important role in the dedication of Grace Methodist Church in 1905 when Pentalpha Lodge officiated at the cornerstone laying. Of course, the Knights of Pythias were also present in a body at the Grace Church dedication. This may have been a time of decision for some because some men belonged to both groups. This is one reason why the two survived the difficult period with such success. Both held human principles of brotherhood, benevolence, friendship, and charity as their first considerations. Neither was an exclusive organization and many of Gaithersburg's leading citizens belonged to both. While the two may have had periods of rivalry, they were friendly competitions that benefited the town and the members.

THE WOMAN'S CLUB OF GAITHERSBURG

The Woman's Club was founded April 15, 1921 and united with the Montgomery County Federation of Woman's Clubs that same year, and with the Maryland State Federation of Woman's Clubs on March 11, 1923.

The charter members consisted of a group of 25 active and 10 associate members. The club met twice a month in the homes of its members. There was a 5¢ fine if late, and membership was limited to 35.

The charter members consisted of a group of women who had worked actively in the Red Cross and other organizations during World War I. The original inspiration and purpose for forming the club was the desire to establish a memorial for the men of the Gaithersburg area who lost their lives in the war. The club raised money and purchased a bronze plaque listing the names of those men. This plaque was placed on the front of the building on the corner of Diamond and Summit Avenues, known then as the "First National Bank of Gaithersburg" building.

On June 23, 1922, the plaque was dedicated with suitable ceremonies by General M.A. Record and Colonel E. Brooke Lee, officers of Maryland forces. A large crowd of interested persons attended and a dinner and reception were held in the evening.

During the early years of the Gaithersburg Woman's Club there were very few civic or charitable organizations in town, so the clubs performed many services and engaged in extensive civic activities. Among these were efforts to improve conditions at the County Alms House and at the jail, and to increase salaries for teachers. At this time there was no high school in the lower part of the county and the club worked for the establishment of the Bethesda High School and also for the employment of a drawing teacher for the county schools. The club also appeared in a body before the Gaithersburg Town Council, stressing the need for town sewers.

The scholarship fund was used by a number of students. Radios were bought for military hospitals. Contributions were made to a fund for the education of war veterans and to help hurricane victims, Montgomery General Hospital, the Social Service League of Montgomery County, and numerous other charities and activities.

These contributions were not only in money, but in physical labor, as members canned fruits and vegetables for the hospital, helped at the hospital suppers, and collected food and clothing, which they took to Glen Echo fire house.

The club entered "The National Rural Better Homes Contest" held by the U.S. government and sponsored by President Herbert Hoover. The club won second prize in the nation and $175, which went into the scholarship fund.

An antique exhibit and tea was held for a week in the historic Clopper-Hutton house as a fund-raiser for the restoration of "Wakefield," the boyhood home of George Washington. Club members exhibited antiques other than those already in the house. The exhibit included guided tours of the house including its secret room. Again $175 was cleared.

The county fair was very much a local affair and was held in Rockville. The club won a prize for showing contrasting back yards: one cluttered and full of trash, the other with a wildflower garden and a home-made bird bath.

The Pythian Sisters of Forest Oak Temple no. 18 were founded in 1919 and reorganized in 1947.

During this period of the club's history, besides the many civic, charitable, and social activities, the group held regular meetings every two weeks in the homes of members. Each member was required to present one paper or program every year.

The club remained very much the same until World War II. During the war and after, Gaithersburg became more a part of suburbia and less a quiet country town, resulting in more people, more organizations, and less personal involvement. The personal element was replaced by paid and trained people and money from community chest and tax funds.

THE GAITHERSBURG HOMEMAKERS CLUB

The Homemakers Club is a member of the Montgomery County Homemakers Clubs, all of which are extension clubs of the University of Maryland. The Gaithersburg Homemakers Club began in 1932 with 12 charter members. A great deal of the group's early activities involved crafts and home improvements.

Early club meetings were held in the homes of members. Typical projects included reed work such as baskets, trays, and footstools, and pictures made by painting scenes on glass, then framing them against a foil back. Lamps, vases, and other objects were decorated or refurbished by pasting colored linings of envelopes on the objects and outlining them with black paint for a stained glass effect. There were also cooking lessons and other household demonstrations and lessons.

The club had about 25 active members in 1978 and met at the Gaithersburg Community Center. Projects included crocheting pearl necklaces and making soap

Work began on the Montgomery County Fairgrounds in 1949.

sculptures and Christmas decorations. The group also made Easter baskets and sent Christmas gifts to Rosewood and Henryton State Hospitals for institutionalized children and adults.

NEIGHBORHOOD GARDEN CLUB

The Gaithersburg-Washington Grove Neighborhood Garden Club had its beginning when a group of 15 ladies, including a few members of a disbanded club from Washington Grove, met on the morning of November 25, 1931 at the Gaithersburg fire house. Mrs. Laura Ann Wadsworth Thompson became the first president. Mrs. Merle Jacobs, Mrs. Lawson King, and Mrs. Thompson were the only surviving charter members in 1978. The purpose of the organization has always been to make the topics of garden and flower arrangement interesting and instructive to each member and to help to beautify the community and surrounding area in any way possible.

In the early days much time was given to discussions of how to plant, what fertilizers to use, and how to care for plants. Speakers gave freely of their time and talents. Many of the plants and trees that were planted then are still growing today. The Neighborhood Garden Club still meets regularly.

By 1940, the town could sense growth on the horizon. The economy was recovering from the Depression years, the Washington area had ample employment, and better roads eased commuting to jobs outside the city. The needs of the citizens now became too great for the mayor and council to handle unassisted. To supplement them, a number of service clubs were formed that made significant contributions to the town's progress and well being.

From 1960 to the present, Gaithersburg completed the change from small town to city suburb in a major metropolitan area. A number of scientific firms were attracted to the area and these in turn brought related service businesses to the town. The rapidly increasing population lured new merchants, doctors, lawyers, and other professionals to the city and these new residents once again brought new tastes, abilities, and interests to the community. A number of personal interest, professional, and hobby groups were formed to share these interests. Culture and entertainment are once again a primary part of life in Gaithersburg.

THE MONTGOMERY COUNTY AGRICULTURAL FAIR

Montgomery County farmers looked to each other for support and for ideas to improve their conditions. Before 1850 farmers began to meet after harvest time in Rockville at the grounds where Richard Montgomery High School is now located in order to measure their progress against each other and to enjoy the fruits of their labors. This became the Montgomery County Agricultural Fair. When the fair outgrew the available land, a 64-acre site was selected in Gaithersburg near the rail line with good road access. It was a part of the Meem farm called Mt. Washington. The Meem's original 1865 home was located on the high knoll at the north end of the site and its name was a pun on the Meem's first names: George and Martha.

After years of planning, construction began on the Montgomery County Cooperative Agricultural Center on June 4, 1949. Between 850 and 1,000 people came that day and completed the buildings in a huge "barn-raising" campaign. Other barns and buildings at the fairgrounds were constructed in a similar style.

The complex is owned and operated by the Montgomery County Agricultural Center, Inc., a non-profit corporation. The bylaws of the corporation were written so that the land cannot be mortgaged for loans and if the property is sold, all proceeds must go to charity. Volunteer labor, interest-free loans from local businessmen, and the profits from the fair have continued to result in the improvement and expansion of the agricultural center over the years. The remainder of the fair profit goes to pay for caretakers, office employees, and the executive director who works closely with the board of directors.

The first fair in Gaithersburg took place in 1949. Admission was 50¢ for adults and 25¢ for children and 12,000 people paid admission that first year. There were many classes and livestock, poultry, farm, and household exhibits. More cows were brought than the exhibition had space for, and prizes awarded amounted to $7,500. Total attendance was 15,000.

In addition to the regular fair exhibits, certain features have developed into regular attractions over the years. In 1962, the U.S. Agriculture Extension Service suggested that the fair observe the 100th anniversary of the Department of Agriculture and the 50th anniversary of the extension service with an exhibit of old-time farm machinery and household items. The exhibit proved so popular that it has been continued ever since. It is now known as the Old Timers exhibit and is located near the main entrance to the fairgrounds.

In 1966, the Gaithersburg Future Farmers of America decided to set up an exhibit of animals with special appeal to youngsters. Old MacDonald's Farm grew from an exhibit in one-third of the dairy barn that first year to the most popular single attraction for fair-goers, with species of dairy and beef cattle, sheep, swine, goats, and rabbits on display.

The Girls 4-H Club department began with the first fair in 1949 as part of the household department. There were four sections: baked goods, food preservation, candies, and clothing. The Boys 4-H Club demonstrations were first held in 1950. In 1971, a new 4-H building was erected to accommodate the indoor exhibits when the 4-H Arts and Crafts Department was organized.

The Home Arts Department has become the largest single department at the fair, with exhibits numbering in the thousands. There are also departments for hobbies, farm and garden, honey and beeswax, and sheep, swine, rabbits, goats, and poultry. There is a well-known horse show during the fair and a special children's day when all children enter free.

The decorative farm mural at the Chestnut Street entrance was created in cooperation with the city in 1990. Standard Supplies donated the wall space and many others contributed time and money. Artist Dean Wroth was commissioned by the city to design the five murals and city staff and volunteers completed the painting in 1994. The original artwork for the five panels was auctioned with the proceeds going to the VIP Children's Day at the fair.

In the late 1980s, a new grandstand was built, and in 1993, the Old Timers exhibit building received a "new" turn-of-the-century general store façade. It has an old gas pump in front, a windmill, and lots of country store items on the shelves. Artisans demonstrate old crafts such as shingle cutting, butter making, spinning, printing, and hand milling wood on an old lathe. The storefront faces the Arts and Craft Building, which was constructed by the Gaithersburg Business Association in 1953 and donated to the Agricultural Center 10 years later.

For the other 51 weeks of the year the center is used regularly for meetings and social activities as well as dog shows, cat shows, garlic shows, craft and antique shows, and other events too varied to list. The fairgrounds are always busy during the winter as well.

The community owes a great debt of gratitude to the volunteers who built this landmark in 1949, and a large group of volunteers still provide fair labor each year. According to Roscoe Whipp, one of the original volunteers, "The focus of the center and the fair has remained the same. It was built for the agricultural youth of Montgomery County, so they could exhibit their animals and their arts and craft projects. The purpose is to help the youth today—it always has been and still is."

Douglas King received a first-prize ribbon from Betty Miles at the 1949 Montgomery County Fair. (Photo by Roscoe Whipp.)

6. Religious Life

Gaithersburg's ministerial association has been active for more than 50 years and acts as an ecumenical council among the city's religious congregations. Long before Gaithersburg became a town, individuals practiced their religions in private homes in the area. As the city grows to include many different cultures, many different religious faiths are represented. Many churches built places of worship in Gaithersburg in the late-nineteenth and twentieth centuries. Today, religious groups also use community facilities such as schools, recreational centers, and meeting rooms to gather.

St. Luke's Presbyterian

St. Luke's Presbyterian Meetinghouse at 446 North Frederick Avenue was the first church structure built in Gaithersburg. Elijah Thompson and his wife, Elizabeth, made a deed on August 2, 1847 with Otho Magruder, Richard Cromwell, and John T. DeSellum "for the purpose of erecting thereon by the Society of Christians called 'Presbyterians' a house of public worship." The meetinghouse was built and owned by the Presbyterians in 1847–1848, but no records of this early congregation exist.

Presbyterians in Montgomery County were served by a pastor on a circuit that included Bethesda, Rockville, and Middlebrook before 1847. After that date, the three churches separated. John DeSellum and Richard Cromwell were elders of the Presbyterian Church and may have continued services at the new meetinghouse, but the Methodist Church soon occupied or perhaps shared the meetinghouse.

When the Baltimore Conference and the Gaithersburg Methodist Episcopal Church were split into north and south congregations in 1861, the north group remained at the Presbyterian Meetinghouse. This congregation was renamed Epworth when it built a new church on Brookes Avenue in 1891. When the meetinghouse was no longer needed by the Methodists, it was sold to Philemon Smith and converted into a residence. The building was demolished in the late 1970s during the widening of Frederick Avenue.

The Gaithersburg Presbyterian Church was established in 1962 with about 40 members who met in temporary quarters until their new building was erected and dedicated at 600 South Frederick Avenue in 1966. The church provides spiritual leadership, social groups, and musical worship groups for all ages. It serves the community through social programs

Epworth Methodist Church was located at 14 Brookes Avenue in the 1920s. (Courtesy of Albert Fulk.)

and a pre-school. It is especially known for sharing cultural and musical presentations with the community. A new addition to the church began in 2001.

THE METHODIST CHURCH IN GAITHERSBURG

The Gaithersburg Methodist Churches stemmed from one of the oldest Methodist classes in America, the Middlebrook class that was led by Thomas English.

"Brother English's" house often served as a place of worship. It was located near the point where Game Preserve Road crosses under Interstate 270. It was one of the original 10 congregations when the Rockville Circuit was formed in 1844 and probably existed before that time. Although the Baltimore Conference of the Methodist Church did not divide until 1861, the Southern Methodists had split from the church in 1845. Maryland's geographical situation during the Civil War prevented any alliances between the Southern and Northern Conferences, and Gaithersburg remained under the Baltimore, and hence Northern Conference. Although the dissension and then the formation of a rival conference was founded upon a chapter of the *Methodist Discipline* that dealt with slavery, the physical division of the Gaithersburg Methodist Episcopal Church occurred after the war was over.

When the Rockville Circuit affiliated with the Methodist Church South in 1866, most of the Middlebrook class was comfortable with the new association. The Gaithersburg families that joined the Southern Conference were the Briggs, Walkers, and Claggets. About 30 others, including the English, Fulks, Crawford, Lemmon, and other families, stayed with the Northern Conference.

GAITHERSBURG AND EPWORTH METHODIST EPISCOPAL CHURCHES

Thomas English and the other trustees of the new Gaithersburg Methodist Episcopal Church paid the Presbyterians $1,000 for St. Luke's Meetinghouse in 1867. The deed indicated the building was to be used as "a place of Divine Worship, for the ministry and membership of the Methodist Episcopal Church in the United States of America." By 1890, the Gaithersburg congregation had become large enough to support a new circuit with the preacher headquartered in Gaithersburg.

The first Methodist Episcopal preacher in Gaithersburg was Reverend R.M. Moore. The congregation also incorporated in 1890. It was growing in number and needed a larger building, so a lot on the newly platted Brookes Avenue was chosen and purchased in 1891. The new frame church was dedicated in 1891 with appropriate fanfare. In 1905, the parsonage at 13 Brookes Avenue was donated by Susan Collins.

Epworth Methodist Episcopal Church established a mission church in 1902 at Hunting Hill, about 4 miles from Gaithersburg. Ignatius Beall Ward and his wife, Elizabeth Garrett Ward, gave land for this chapel on what is now 10315 Darnestown Road, not far from

These children are rehearsing a program at the old Epworth Methodist Church in 1948. (Courtesy of Betty Jeanne Jacobs.)

McDonald Chapel, the mission church founded by members of the Methodist Episcopal Church South.

Epworth's parent conference purchased land in 1872 and established the Washington Grove Camp Grounds in 1873. (It is now the Town of Washington Grove.) Washington Grove was planned as a summer retreat for religious instruction and entertainment. The camp offered a special Epworth League Day for young people and a Chautauqua was frequently held as a part of the annual meeting. The Chautauqua involved special guest lecturers on a variety of topics both intellectual and religious. The idea had spread from a Sunday School Teacher Assembly held at Chautauqua Lake, New York in 1874 and seemed to reach its height in the early 1900s. This was in addition to the Sunday school, the Epworth League, the Ladies Aid Society, and the regular services produced by Epworth.

In 1938, an addition was built on the rear of the church on Brookes Avenue. A large auditorium with a stage, kitchen, and a smaller meeting room were added. In the aftermath of the 1939 unification of the Methodist Episcopal Church and the Methodist Episcopal Church South, Epworth became Epworth Methodist Church of the Washington West District of the Baltimore Conference. Organ chimes were presented in 1943 by Mr. and Mrs. J. Wriley Jacobs in memory of their parents and were dedicated on September 5. In 1948, the sanctuary was completely remodeled at a cost of $10,000 and reopened on Sunday, October 24, 1948.

On January 17, 1955, the first committee to search for a new site for Epworth Church was appointed. A study recommending the purchase of a site located at Rosemont Drive and South Frederick Avenue (Route 355) was approved by the Quarterly Conference. The congregation voted to purchase the site for the new church on June 15, 1958. The church was completed in 1963 and was dedicated on January 19, 1964, with Bishop John Wesley Lord of the Washington Area of the Methodist Church officiating. An education wing was dedicated in 1981.

The ministry of the church continued to change and grow as Gaithersburg and its surrounding area changed. In addition to a pre-school, a before- and after-school child-care program and an after-school Hispanic tutorial were begun. A volunteer-run thrift shop served the community, as did an office of the Gaithersburg Pastoral Counseling Center. Epworth continues its programs of nurture and service with regular worship, Sunday school, youth groups, children's choirs, bell choirs, a youth choir, and a chancel choir. Men's, women's, youth, and multi-generational groups continue active, hands-on service within the church and the extended community.

FOREST OAK METHODIST EPISCOPAL CHURCH SOUTH

Since the Methodists did not own the Presbyterian Meetinghouse in 1866, the South members built a new church called the Forest Oak Methodist Episcopal Church South two blocks south on what is now the cemetery. At that time the U.S. Post Office was located in the Forest Oak Store and Forest Oak was the local mailing address. The North group purchased the meetinghouse and remained the Gaithersburg Methodist Episcopal Church so the new church was named "Forest Oak."

In 1866, the trustees of the new Forest Oak Methodist Episcopal Church South purchased land from Elijah Thompson to be used for a church and a burial ground. This was the first burial ground purchased by the Methodist Episcopal Church South in Montgomery County. It is likely that this land was used as a burial ground even before the Church purchased it, as several markers have death dates antedating the 1866 purchase. Therefore, it seems plausible that the reason the deed specifically mentioned a burial ground was because the property was already in use as a cemetery. At any rate, Elijah Thompson himself was buried in the cemetery only a year after he sold it to the church, and from then on it was used as the church burial ground.

The congregation donated labor, and the handsome new frame church house was dedicated on November 17, 1867 with about 60 members. It continued to grow and the church was expanded and remodeled in 1884. In 1887, the Gaithersburg Methodist Episcopal Church South was large enough to support its own circuit. The Gaithersburg Circuit included the Darnestown, Travilah, Boyds, and Germantown Methodist Episcopal South churches. The McDonald Chapel at Quince Orchard was built in 1901.

In 1878, an additional 1.1 acres to the rear of the church were conveyed to the trustees of the Methodist Episcopal Church South by Thomas and Matilda Lanahan to be used as a burial ground. On June 2, 1879, a group of churchmen formed a cemetery association to manage the enlarged burial ground. The organization was an operating group only and no provision was made for perpetual care. An initial modest payment was required for opening a grave on the lot. Money from sales was used for keeping up the property.

In 1893, the Methodist Episcopal Church South in Gaithersburg incorporated and the church and churchyard was transferred to the corporation. When the Forest Oak congregation decided to move from the old church and build a new Methodist Episcopal Church South on the corner of Walker and Frederick Avenue, the old Forest Oak Church was sold to Alexander G. Carlisle. Carlisle dismantled it and used the stained-glass windows, door, and window frames on his new funeral parlor and furniture store on Diamond Avenue. This doubled the size of the cemetery.

Grace United Methodist Church

The new church was built on 0.825 acres of land purchased for $100 from two church members, Carson and Carrie Ward. It was on the corner of John Walker's farm lane and subdivision, which soon became a Methodist Church South. The materials were stone for the base, brick and cedar shingles for the exterior, fine slate for the roof, oak pews and furniture, and large stained-glass windows. The final cost of the church was reported at $17,500 and it was named Grace. It was dedicated on May 20, 1905 when all stores in town closed, and Governor Warfield participated in the ceremonies officiated by Gaithersburg's Pentalpha Lodge of Masons.

The congregation dug out the basement for a community room in 1919, sold the church parsonage at 11 Chestnut in 1923, and built a new one behind the church at 1 Walker Avenue. This parsonage was demolished in 1982 to build the Walker Building after the congregation decided to refurbish and enlarge the old church rather than sell and build anew elsewhere. The new wing included a new community hall, offices, and classrooms.

Grace and its leadership played a crucial role establishing and building the Asbury Methodist Home in Gaithersburg as a home for older members of the conference. The Methodist Church reunited in 1939 and merged with the Evangelical United Brethren Church in 1968. Grace officially became Grace United Methodist Church. It is known for its daily carillon music and the beautiful stained-glass windows dedicated as memorials to the founders of the church.

FOREST OAK CEMETERY

The Forest Oak Cemetery remained under the care of the Forest Oak and Grace Church for a time, then became a community facility. In 1906, the town passed a law saying, "It shall not be lawful . . . to establish a cemetery or burial ground within the limits of the Town of Gaithersburg, Maryland, without the consent of the Mayor and Council." This law gave the Forest Oak Cemetery a monopoly in town.

John Wesley Walker and George Walker owned land directly adjacent to the church cemetery, which was also used as a burial ground. Lots were purchased from the Walkers rather than from the church. In 1915, John Wesley Walker and his wife donated 10,494 square feet along Frederick Avenue to the cemetery association, "for a term which shall continue so long only as the present ordinance of the Town of Gaithersburg prohibiting the interment of bodies therein remains in full force." At the same time the widow and children of George Walker donated exactly the same amount of land along Frederick

Pictured here is the bell tower of Grace United Methodist Church, which was built in 1905.

Dr. Elisha Cornelius Etchison's 1879 house was located next door to the present-day Grace Methodist Church.

Avenue to the association under the same conditions. These two transfers from the Walkers tripled the frontage of the cemetery on Frederick Avenue.

In 1910, the Forest Oak Cemetery Association incorporated separately. The property was operated by the cemetery association from 1910 onwards but was officially transferred to the Forest Oak Cemetery Association in 1934. In 1911, the town held Decoration Day exercises at the cemetery. In the mid-1920s, an ornamental metal fence was purchased of such outstanding quality that it is still standing today. Dr. E.C. Etchison donated the wrought-iron gates, which were once at the monumental entrance to his property. A fine wrought-iron sign was placed over the gate with the words "Forest Oak Cemetery." In the 1960s, it became necessary to widen the entrance to the cemetery. The fence was retained but the gates donated by the Etchison family were too narrow for the new entrance, so they were stored and eventually returned to the Etchison family. The familiar overhead sign was refurbished by the Lions Club and placed, with a new inscription, at the entrance to Duvall Park.

When Frederick Avenue was widened in 1980, 111 graves were omitted and the old fence had to be removed. After much deliberation, the board of directors voted to restore and replace the original ornamental fence.

The cemetery continues to be operated by the Forest Oak Cemetery Association, which is controlled by a volunteer board of directors. In 1989, the association bylaws were changed to allow a fund to ensure the financial security of the cemetery. Today, the association is a tax-exempt corporation and accepts donations for the perpetual care of the cemetery.

The early Methodist classes were not officially segregated by race before the Civil War. In 1864, before the end of the war, Baltimore Conference records indicate that there were 320 whites and 160 African Americans in the circuit churches. Following the war, there were 340 whites and no African Americans. In the United States in general, African-American Methodists formed their own churches after the war. This was the case in the Gaithersburg area as well.

PLEASANT VIEW METHODIST CHURCH

The three Quince Orchard churches represented the three different directions taken by the Gaithersburg Methodists. Pleasant View, the first of the three, was begun by African-American Methodists in 1868 when Thomas Neverson, George W. Johnson, and Charles Beander bought land and an old building on Darnestown Road to begin a Methodist Episcopal Church. The first Pleasant View church was not built until 1888. John Ricks was the local minister, and church leaders were Samuel Neverson and Andrew Jenkins. Vernon Green served as chairman of the trustees of the early church, frequently referred to as the Quince Orchard Church.

By 1914, the old Pleasant View church was in such poor condition that it was razed and rebuilt. Members attended services in Quince Orchard Colored School in the interim. At various times, the church was held with the Washington Grove Church, the Scotland Church, the Emory Grove Church, or with the Linden Church. The Quince Orchard Church initiated an extensive building campaign in the mid-1950s. A pastor's study, a choir room and choir loft, and an oil burner to replace the old coal stove were added. In 1955, running water was installed in the parish house, formerly the Quince Orchard Colored School; two restrooms were added; and a new organ and pulpit were purchased.

McDONALD CHAPEL

The second Quince Orchard church was started toward the end of the nineteenth century when Reverend Louis L. Lloyd of the Forest Oak Methodist Episcopal Church South also began holding services near the corner of Quince Orchard and Darnestown Roads. The Forest Oak trustees purchased part of the property of William Small for the construction of a new church. Their new minister in 1899 was William A. McDonald, who labored long and hard to see the church built. He died before construction was completed in 1903 and the church was named McDonald Chapel in his honor. In 1907, after Forest Oak was succeeded by Grace Methodist Episcopal Church South, the property was formally turned over to the McDonald Chapel trustees.

McDonald Chapel grew slowly and remained on a charge with Grace Church for 50 years, until 1955. During that time, work was completed on a church basement for classroom use. The Ladies Aid Society had become inactive but a Women's Society was organized and a Methodist Youth Fellowship was formed.

HUNTING HILL METHODIST EPISCOPAL CHURCH

The third Quince Orchard church was a mission started in 1902 at Hunting Hill by Epworth Methodist Episcopal Church. Originally known as Mizpah Church, it was located where Key West Avenue and Route 28 merge, on land donated by Ignatius Beall Ward and his wife, Elizabeth Garrett Ward. The lumber for the building was brought up Route 28 from a Rockville church that was being torn down, and the chapel was built in the mission-house style. In memory of Mrs. Ward's mother, the family donated stained-glass windows, each inscribed, "In memory of Frances Garrett."

Originally, Hunting Hill was on a charge with its parent Epworth Church, and for a time it was on a charge with Eldbrooke Church in Tenleytown, Washington, D.C. Under the leadership of Reverend Louis A. Mossburg (1924–1925), a parish hall was built. The hall was the scene of many famous suppers given by the ladies with help from the men of the church. They served four or five suppers a year, even though water had to be carried from a nearby home. The suppers helped the church to meet its financial obligations for many years. Following an especially successful ham and oyster supper in the 1950s, the parish hall caught fire and was partially destroyed. It was rebuilt and redecorated however, with most of the expenses covered by insurance.

FAIRHAVEN UNITED METHODIST CHURCH

By 1960, the three churches were struggling. Despite the differences in their roots, one from the Northern Methodist Episcopal Church, one from the Methodist Episcopal Church South, and the other with nearly a century of history as an African-American Methodist Church, there were some similarities. All had less than 100 members. McDonald Chapel had 91, Hunting Hill, 55, and Pleasant View, 50. Their buildings were old, and none had land for future expansion. The few leaders were spread over many positions. The times were changing, and the divisions of the past were beginning to weigh heavily on the torn cloth of the Methodist Church. The Baltimore Conference merged with the African-American Washington Conference in 1965, although individual churches remained highly segregated.

Both McDonald Chapel and Hunting Hill had been placed on the same charge with Washington Grove Methodist Church in 1955. Then, in 1958, Washington Grove became an independent church, leaving Hunting Hill and McDonald Chapel sharing Reverend William Nukols, who had just been discharged from the armed forces and was attending Wesley Seminary in Washington, D.C.

In 1960, it was mentioned that there was the possibility of merging the three churches. Although an attempt to merge the two white churches failed in 1962, the two did jointly provide an apartment for their minister. In 1962, Reverend Kenneth Carder, also a Wesley Seminary student, became the pastor for the Hunting Hill/McDonald Chapel charge. On the basis of an extensive study of membership, leadership, finances, attendance, facilities, and growth in the community, it was recommended in spring 1965 that the churches merge administratively but operate both facilities until a new church location could be found and the congregations begin seriously considering how best to relate to the Pleasant View Methodist Church.

Forest Oak Church was established in 1866.

Both congregations together were able to build and quickly pay for a parsonage. In May 1965, following long and difficult deliberations but an almost unanimous vote, McDonald Chapel and Hunting Hill formally filed documents of merger. It was difficult to give up the traditions ingrained for so many years and a few members left. Eventually Hunting Hill Church went unused and was sold to Central Baptist Church. Reverend Carder came up with the idea for the name of the combined church, Fairhaven, which was accepted by the congregation.

Pleasant View had been in a charge relationship with Emory Grove Methodist Church, sharing a minister appointed under the segregated central jurisdiction. Then the Methodist Church abolished the central jurisdiction and the official written policy was to be "the absence on all levels of church life of patterns and policies based on color."

In October 1967, Bishop John Wesley Lord came to Fairhaven and Pleasant View and preached that the barrier of race should be broken down. The congregations of Fairhaven and Pleasant View left familiar territory and ventured into the unknown as pilgrims. They had been discussing a possible merger. These discussions, especially those of a small group known as the "Group of Concerned Christians," eventually led the two congregations to join together. At their meeting in September 1968, they agreed to trust each other and examine the possibilities for the future.

Avoiding the problems of another merger, the unification of the African-American and white churches was accomplished by transferring the memberships of most of the

Pleasant View congregation to Fairhaven on several Sundays in September 1968. A few members of Pleasant View decided not to join Fairhaven but services were discontinued at Pleasant View on September 29, 1968. In essence, the Pleasant View congregation, by joining Fairhaven, left their church and their previous positions yet brought their heritage, music, and leadership, all of which would re-emerge in Fairhaven. Their initiative a decade earlier to develop leadership culminated in the unification of the churches, and this leadership continued in enriching Fairhaven. In the years following this unification, the fabric of the church has been rewoven into a new cloth of many colors. A new church community was formed out of a Southern Methodist church, a Northern Methodist church, and an African-American Methodist church.

The old Pleasant View church is the only one of the three original buildings still standing. The church and the old Quince Orchard School have been designated the Pleasant View Historic District and are on the "County Master Plan for Historic Preservation." The Hunting Hill Church was sold, but the building was later torn down to make way for Key West Boulevard. McDonald Chapel was razed despite the protests of some historic preservationists in the county. A street from the site into a new housing development has been named McDonald Chapel Drive.

ASCENSION EPISCOPAL CHURCH

In 1880, the vestry of Prince George's Episcopal parish decided that another chapel was needed along the Frederick Road. The chapel committee persuaded John and Sarah

Ascension Chapel was completed in 1882 in a simple meetinghouse style.

DeSellum to donate land at the corner of Summit and Frederick Avenues and raised funds. The simple frame meetinghouse-style building was completed in 1882 and dedicated in 1885. Until 1950, the Rockville church served the congregation. In 1955, the congregation separated the chapel from the parish and became a diocesan mission. The first full-time clergyman was hired in 1960. Church membership has increased dramatically and the church purchased and removed the two Victorian houses next to it to build a new house of worship. The original church has been converted into church offices and meeting space. Ascension Episcopal Church is the oldest church still standing in Gaithersburg.

St. Martin of Tours Catholic Church

In the 1880s, Gaithersburg Catholics worshipped at the Samuel and Rebecca Gloyd home at 5 North Frederick Avenue, where a room was set aside as a chapel. In 1914, eight ladies of the church set out to acquire the site of the former Summit Hotel as a permanent location for worship.

According to the church history, *65 Years of Ministry*, John B. Diamond, a Catholic, donated his share of the property and Mr. Fulks sold his interest in the land for half its value. The land became the property of the Archdiocese of Baltimore under the supervision of Father George Harrington, pastor of St. Mary's Church in Barnesville. Father Harrington was succeeded by Father John S. Cuddy before any definite building plans were made.

Father Cuddy was from Baltimore. His legacy to Gaithersburg is his name on the railroad overpass on Frederick Avenue, two blocks north of St. Martin's Church. In 1928, Father Cuddy was struck by a railroad train and killed at this intersection. His death raised such an outcry that the crossing was identified as one of the most dangerous in the state and the overpass was built shortly after. A two-lane bridge was dedicated in 1930, which was taken down and rebuilt as a six-lane bridge during the widening of Frederick Avenue in 1987.

Initially Mass and Sunday school were held in surplus U.S. Army mess halls moved to the site. St Martin's Roman Catholic School, the first Catholic parochial school in the county, was built in 1925. The rectory was erected in 1934 during the tenure of Father Callaghan (1928–1935), who succeeded Father Cuddy. This eliminated the need for priests to board with parishioners in the community.

According to George Gartner, a lifelong member of St. Martin's, the rectory was home to St. Martin's priests and their housekeepers. Meetings were held in the parlor and small religious education classes were held in the basement. The church office was also in the basement. The parish built a new house for its clergy across Frederick Avenue on DeSellum Avenue in 1995, and the rectory is now used exclusively as the parish office.

The Baptist Church

The oldest Baptist Church in the Gaithersburg area is the African-American Baptist Church located at Poplar Grove. In 1893, a new church was built further down the highway on a tract of land owned by a Mr. Gray. Several ministers served the log cabin Poplar Grove Baptist Church. Reverend James E. Prather made many improvements to the church in the 1960s and 1970s.

Until 1955, other Baptists in Gaithersburg held memberships in churches elsewhere. On May 15, 1955, 20 people established a Baptist Church in Gaithersburg at the Gaither Theater. Since that day, a regular schedule of services has been conducted by the First Baptist Church. In June 1955, the church moved to the Masonic Temple in Gaithersburg. In the fall of 1955, the congregation purchased 8 acres on West Diamond Avenue to build a sanctuary and educational building. Ground was broken in 1961 and the building was dedicated in April 1962. Another addition was made in 1978 and a new sanctuary was completed in December 2000.

OTHER PLACES OF WORSHIP

Many other denominations and religions came to Gaithersburg over the past 30 years and continue to practice their faiths in places of worship today.

The Gaithersburg Mennonite Church started in 1953 at the corner of Summit Hall Road and Water Street. In 1956, a church building was erected at 19 Mills Road off Water Street.

The First Assembly of God congregation was organized in 1956 by Reverend Milton Ross. A plot of land was purchased and a small church was built at Cedar Avenue and Deer Park Drive.

The Lutheran people of Gaithersburg also wanted to have their own church. In April 1964, a group of 14 interested Lutherans met to consider the best method of organizing. Meetings were held in the fall of 1964 and the name Good Shepherd Lutheran Church was chosen. Ground for the church was purchased on South Frederick Avenue and the building was dedicated on June 28, 1969. A new building was completed in 1978.

Jewish residents of Gaithersburg worshiped together for the first time on February 19, 1971 at Watkins Mill Elementary School. Gaithersburg Hebrew Congregation was the first synagogue in the upper Interstate 270 corridor. In 1977, a synagogue-religious school was built on Apple Ridge Road.

In 1974, the Baha'i Faith came to Gaithersburg, which had been selected from among 12 other cities as the location for a new Baha'i Community.

In 1977, the Church of Jesus Christ of Latter Day Saints located in the Gaithersburg area and completed its meetinghouse in 1979 on Apple Ridge Road. Another church was formed in the Kentlands around 1994.

7. THE BALTIMORE & OHIO RAILROAD

When Gaithersburg was a hamlet of only three or four houses, it owed its existence to the road between the District of Columbia and the lands being opened beyond the Alleghenies. It was dependent on this road for the travelers' business and for shipping its profitable tobacco crop to market. The town grew as transportation improved, and the region was always eager for new and better ways to travel and ship goods. On July 4, 1828, in simultaneous ceremonies in Baltimore and on the banks of the Potomac at Little Falls, work officially began on construction of the Baltimore & Ohio Railroad and the Chesapeake & Ohio Canal. Both ventures held the promise of swift advances in agriculture and trade, but both followed courses far away from Gaithersburg and other towns in central Montgomery County.

The merchants of Georgetown feared that Baltimore was gaining a commercial advantage against which they could not compete. Accordingly, they made common cause with Montgomery County leaders and proposed to build a line of their own, the Metropolitan Railroad, which would run through Montgomery County to Point of Rocks, where it would connect with the B&O.

They enlisted the support of two of Montgomery County's leading citizens, Francis Cassatt Clopper of Gaithersburg and General William Lingan Gaither, a member of the Maryland Senate. In early 1853, application was made to the Maryland legislature for a charter. Senator Gaither was an influential advocate, and the bill quickly passed the senate.

The first meeting of incorporators on July 30, 1853 included General Gaither, Francis Clopper, and Robert T. Dade of Montgomery County. On August 3, officers and directors were chosen, with Clopper as the Montgomery County representative. A week later, a chief engineer was selected, and on August 22, field work began for the survey to select the "most eligible and central route" from Georgetown to the west.

The line finally chosen conforms closely to that which the B&O follows today through Montgomery County. Unhappily, this central route did not please the citizens of Frederick and Washington Counties, for it ran far west of the line they favored. Public sentiment in the two counties turned against the Metropolitan, and all hope of financial aid from those quarters vanished. Indeed, from that time forward their representatives in the general assembly joined Baltimore in opposing actions favorable to the Metropolitan Railroad.

Time was running out. Its charter gave the Metropolitan two years, until May 5, 1855, to start work, and until 1858 to complete it. To save the charter, the company awarded a contract to John S. Christie & Co. for 20 miles of grading, masonry, and bridging along the selected route. Work began on April 10, 1855, 25 days before the charter would otherwise have expired. This action effectively extended the company's life until April 10, 1860.

A bill to accomplish this, and to give the company until 1863 to complete the work, was introduced by General Gaither, by that time president of the senate. The senate passed the bill on February 19 with only three dissenting votes, and it cleared the house of delegates a few days later.

With this new lease on life, the company authorized Clopper on March 4 to seek additional stock subscriptions. Clopper worked hard to stimulate sales, writing persuasive letters to editors and men of affairs. Rockville's leading newspaper, the *Sentinel*, carried favorable comments on the railroad and gave prominent space to an unabashed and lengthy essay purportedly from "a friend in Frederick County" urging Montgomery farmers to invest in the line because of the enhanced value it would bring to their property holdings. Most important, Clopper wrote to Chauncy Brooks, president of the B&O, arguing eloquently that the Metropolitan line presented such benefits to the B&O that the latter ought to take positive advantage of it rather than opposing it in Congress and elsewhere. He suggested that the B&O ought to consider building a connecting link between Laurel and Gaithersburg to handle high-speed traffic the old "main stem" could

Coal-burning passenger and freight locomotives like this one made frequent stops at the Gaithersburg station in the early 1900s.

not accommodate. If the B&O wanted to share in the profits of the Metropolitan, Clopper wrote, it was welcome to purchase stock in the company, even a controlling interest. At the very least, he concluded, the B&O should work with the new line for mutual benefit.

But the B&O was in no condition to undertake new ventures and this proposed line was never built. The company's energies were engaged in a furious competitive scramble with the railroads of New York and Pennsylvania for routes to the Midwest. Strikes by railroad workers turned violent in May 1857, with strikers firing on trains. Troops were called in to do battle with the strikers at Baltimore and Ellicott Mills. Finally, the Panic of 1857 was about to start and the nation's railroads, nearly all of them seriously overextended financially, were at the center of the storm. Plans for the Metropolitan and the Laurel-Gaithersburg lines were allowed to slide and were not revived until well into the Civil War.

The Confederate invasion of Maryland in September 1862 caused enormous shock in the nation's capital, awakening the city to its vulnerable position and the strategic importance of a line such as Clopper had been proposing for nearly a decade. A week after Southern troops crossed the Potomac and seized Sugarloaf Mountain, a joint resolution was introduced in the Washington city council urging the immediate construction of rail lines east to Chesapeake and west to Hagerstown as "vitally necessary to the permanent security and prosperity of Washington."

A few days later, Mayor Wallach and a delegation of municipal officers called on President Lincoln to present their resolution and urge federal action. The Washington *Star* reported their proposal "met with the President and Secretary of War." And indeed Lincoln did support the plan in a message to Congress in January 1863. But the terror of 1862 had long abated, and Congress didn't get around to authorizing such a line until July 1, 1864. By this time the original Metropolitan charter had lapsed, and new charters were required.

At its next session early in 1865, the Maryland legislature granted the necessary charter to the B&O. Detailed planning for the route now called the "Metropolitan" Branch in recognition of the contribution of Clopper and his associates began at once.

Expressing its satisfaction with the route chosen, the *Star* noted that it traversed "a region of country admirably adapted for fine building sites, running through a fertile and healthful tract, abounding in those graceful swells and elevations so much sought for private residences of the better class. We have no doubt that the road will, ere many years, be lined with first class country residences for many miles out."

Real progress didn't begin until 1868–1869. A long series of legal actions on February 10, 1868 condemned property along the right-of-way in Montgomery County. In the vicinity of Gaithersburg, the area between the Germantown-Neelsville Road and Washington Grove, ten property owners had lands taken: Henry B. Waring, William Musser, Douglass Clopper, William McConvey (or McConway), Cecelia A. Fitzgerald, Mary R. Bibb, Martha A. Meem, John T. DeSellum, Nathan Cook, and John A. Clements. They were awarded a total of $5,214 for their lands. Additional parcels were taken in June from Eden Gloyd, Elizabeth R. Howard, Ann M. Spates, Elizabeth Read, Thomas Suter, and Rachel Belmear, for which the owners were awarded $9,350.

Several citizens, among them the aging Francis C. Clopper and Charles Saffell, did not go through condemnation proceedings but instead deeded property to the railroad, in

Clopper's case, for a nominal sum plus agreement on the part of the B&O to construct a station and turnout siding on his property.

Construction of the railroad brought a surge of new people to Gaithersburg and other communities along the projected line. Twenty new households comprising a total of 131 individuals were established between the edge of town and Seneca Creek by the time of the 1870 census. This was more than twice as many new residents as the total population counted in that sector within a mile of the center of Gaithersburg.

The newcomers were a cosmopolitan lot. Many were new immigrants from Ireland and Germany, others came from Pennsylvania and Illinois. Some of the African-American workers came from Virginia and South Carolina, though most were Marylanders. Work continued at a quickened pace through 1870 and 1871. As 1872 began, there was considerable hope that the line might be completed by that summer. By the end of March, track had been laid to within 6 miles of Rockville, while crews working from the other end had bridged the Monocacy River and were pushing on in the direction of Gaithersburg. Articles in the *Sentinel* expressed a mixture of elation at the road's progress and irritation that it was taking so long.

A letter in the *Sentinel* praising the enterprise recalled the part played by Francis Clopper in bringing it about: "I am quite cheered that this great work will be completed at an early day," its author wrote. "The memory of the venerable Francis C. Clopper is fondly

This is a photograph of the B&O line at the turn of the twentieth century.

cherished by us as a pioneer of the Metropolitan Railroad. He labored long and hard, with skill and perseverance, until successful. The road was commenced, but he died soon after. He still lives in our hearts as a public benefactor."

Rail service of a sort actually began in July 1872, almost a year before the final completion of the line. An experimental run between Rockville and Washington was made July 22. "The trip about 15 miles was made in an hour, the road not being ballasted, and the whole party were much delighted," the *Sentinel* reported.

Hopes alternately rose and fell. With heavy sarcasm, the editor of the *Sentinel* complained in January 1873 about the slow progress of the rail line. In fact, though the *Sentinel*'s editor was unable to see it, substantial progress was finally being made and the shift of workmen to Gaithersburg was a long stride toward completion of the line. This was made clear just weeks later in the following dispatch:

> The last rail was laid on the Metropolitan B.R.R. at about 1 o'clock, on Saturday last [February 8, 1873]. The forces employed, one of 95 men, at this end of the road, under the management of Mr. Shauen, and the other force of about 200 men, from the Monocacy end, under the management of Mr. Collins, met on that day at Gaithersburg. As the parties neared each other the contest as to which should lay the last rail became more exciting, and never did men move more actively and muscle more briskly, to gain the honor of laying the last rail, and the credit was awarded to the force under Mr. Shauen who reached the goal about two seconds ahead of the other when a shout went up that made the welkin ring. The ballasting on the road has been completed between Washington and Rockville at this end of the road, and from Point of Rocks to the Monocacy at the other end; leaving only the distance between the latter point and Rockville to be ballasted. We have only to say now to Mr. Garrett to "hurry up the cars," and hasten the work to its final completion. The public had become impatient at the long delay, but are now becoming cheered at the prospect of soon realizing their long-cherished hopes. The intimation is given that trains may be in readiness to move passengers to the Inauguration on the 4th of March.

At last, on May 25, this work was done and the first regular service began. "The great work has been accomplished," the *Sentinel* exulted. "Our people may bid farewell to slow coaches and muddy roads. They can now be in Washington in forty-five minutes at a cost of sixty cents. This is much gain in time and money, to the traveling public, while to the farmers along the line, its advantages are incalculable."

Almost overnight the new Metropolitan Branch supplanted the old "main stem" of the B&O as the principal route to the west from Baltimore. As Clopper and Latrobe had foreseen, its easy curves and straightaways made it far more efficient than the twisting course of the earlier line.

Gaithersburg grew rapidly in size. Just five years after the coming of the railroad, the town established its own local government. The town center shifted from the Frederick Road to Diamond Avenue near the rail station. A large frame building, three stories high, was erected to serve as a hotel. A bakery operated by C.F. Hogan, a livery stable run by

John W. Case, and other service establishments rose near the depot. Schools as well as businesses were drawn to locations convenient to the railroad.

Commercial mills, powered by coal-fed steam engines rather than tumbling streams, sprang up along the tracks at many places including Gaithersburg. Trade and commerce flourished all along the line. It became fashionable for city people to go to the country to escape Washington summers, and spacious farmhouses, a mark of their owners' new prosperity, were built with rooms for summer lodgers. Church organizations purchased country tracts, among them the Methodists who bought 250 acres of land near Gaithersburg for residences and a permanent meeting ground.

For a long time most towns along the railroad had only platforms or lightly constructed waiting sheds to accommodate passengers. This may have been a consequence of the 1873–1877 slump, for station houses built during this time were nearly always much smaller and simpler than those projected at the time the rail line was being built.

Gaithersburg's first railway station was established by Walter Talbott in September 1872, more than six months before full service began on the Metropolitan Branch. Shipments must have been small and sporadic, and there is no evidence that a station house existed on the site. The first depot building was erected in 1873 just west of Summit Avenue in the area between the railroad tracks and Diamond Avenue, i.e., across the street from where the present station stands.

Curiously it was the enterprising Talbott, not the B&O, that owned the property. He purchased two adjoining plots in April 1873 from John T. DeSellum and Charles Saffell for $375 and erected a station house and warehouse on the property. A year later he sold the land and facilities to mill owner Upton Darby and partner for $3,200. When they in turn decided to sell, they advertised it as "the best business station on the Metropolitan Branch," noting "over 800 tons of fertilizer alone passed through this Depot last year." Considering Upton Darby's later career with the Gaithersburg Milling and Manufacturing Company, it is hard to understand what made him give up this prosperous agency. Possibly this was also a consequence of the severe economic depression then gripping the country, for the new owner J. Sprigg Poole got the depot at the bargain price of $2,750 compared with the $3,500 that had been asked. Poole became the B&O agent at Gaithersburg, a post that seems to have been much sought after. He built a granary adjacent to the depot and by about 1884 was shipping 100,000 bushels of grain annually.

The present station house, a one-story brick structure about 56 by 22 feet, was built in 1884 on a plot on the east side of Summit Avenue purchased by the railroad from William R. Hutton and Mary Augusta Hutton. The B&O annual report that year characterized the new station as "commodious, substantial and attractive . . . and with all modem conveniences for the comfort of passengers and for the safety of freights." On July 25, 1884, the *Sentinel* recorded in its Gaithersburg column, "The B&O Railroad Company has erected a handsome brick passenger depot at this place. It was much needed and adds much to the place." The women's waiting room was on the west, the agent's office in the middle, and the men's waiting room was on the east. This elegant structure was proof that Gaithersburg was a major station at the time it was built, for only major stations were constructed of brick. Additions to the original structure were made in 1905 and 1907.

This photograph, taken by Tim Smith, shows the Gaithersburg train station.

Although this was by far the most important station serving Gaithersburg people, it was not the only one. Ward's Station on Chestnut Street was named for merchant Henry C. Ward who lived nearby. It had a 9-by-13-foot waiting shed for passengers. A mile farther west was Brown's Station, established in 1894 on the property of Thomas J. and Caroline M. Bibb Brown, who were trying to set up a residential subdivision in the area. On the outskirts of town where Game Preserve Road crosses the railroad was Clopper's Station, built on land given by Francis Clopper shortly before his death.

The B&O had its own telegraph system until 1887 when the railroad sold its equipment to Western Union. The Gaithersburg stationmaster's duties included sending telegraph messages for the public to all points along the B&O. "The public can now telegraph night messages to all points on the B&O and National Company's lines for one cent per word. The B&O has greatly extended its lines and connections in all parts of the country, thus affording quicker, cheaper and more direct telegraph communication than ever before offered by any other company. The rate between all B&O offices in Maryland and West Virginia is 25 cents for 10 words."

The Wye, or "Y," siding that extends from the Metropolitan tracks into the property abutting East Cedar and Frederick Avenues, was built about 1889, with improvements made in 1906, and served as a turnaround for local service to and from Washington. It was designated by the City of Gaithersburg as a local historic site, but later the tracking was removed and the site was paved for parking. The Wye may yet be used for transportation

The freight house serves as the location of the Gaithersburg Community Museum.

in the twentieth century. The Olde Towne Revitalization Plan calls for a linking road from West Diamond to Cedar Avenue to traverse the Wye and directly connect Olde Towne to the Interstate 270 access.

By 1891, the erstwhile village had become a bustling town. John T. DeSellum testified warmly to the changes wrought by the railroad in a letter written shortly before his death:

> The mutual relations of railroads and farmers' interests are shown by the increased value of lands bordering the Metropolitan Branch. This road was located through the most barren part of Montgomery County. Today the improved farms, numerous fine buildings, increased travel and facilities of transportation astonish and delight the beholder.
>
> But I must be brief, and for example can only refer to the material prosperity of Gaithersburg. This formerly humble village, situated in the centre of our county, has since the completion of the railroad developed a trade and importance hitherto thought impossible. More wheat is now annually delivered here than was formerly grown in the whole county. Recently the third Building Association has been organized, with $40,000 taken in $100 shares, a National Bank, with $50,000, and a syndicate with capital of a like amount. The latter designed the erection of a merchant mill of 150 barrels daily capacity, and will deal in cereals, fertilizers, agricultural implements, lumber, coal, etc.

So progressive indeed were the farmers and merchants of Gaithersburg that this community was the first in all Montgomery County to install that new technological marvel of the age, the telephone. Just as it already symbolized the town's connecting link to the outside world by rail and telegraph, the railway station was initially chosen as the site of the telephone switchboard. A.F. Meem, then the B&O stationmaster, founded the telephone company. Frank Farrell was its only employee, working as manager, operator, lineman, and trouble-shooter combined. Initially there were just five lines, connecting the rail station with the bank, the mill, Carson Ward's store, and John B. Diamond's home, and a "long line" to Watkins's store in Travilah, 7 miles distant. But operations expanded rapidly, and the company grew too large to continue at the railway station.

The availability of rapid, easy, frequent transport brought profound changes in lifestyles and outlooks. As early as 1886 the Washington *Star* noted increasing numbers of people using the trains to commute from the countryside to jobs in Washington. Gaithersburg had also become a summer resort. "Many people during the camp meeting season, which is in August, make their headquarters in Gaithersburg," the *Star* reported, noting that the town possessed "a hotel and number of houses where summer guests find homes." The social and cultural activities reported in the county press make it clear that Gaithersburg citizens were becoming more cosmopolitan and sophisticated.

Trains were frequent. In 1891, there were more than a dozen each way daily between Gaithersburg and Washington, beginning at 6:30 in the morning and leaving Washington as late as 11:35 p.m. But there were many accidents and delays too, and a great deal of grumbling on the part of commuters and editorial writers, some of whom sound remarkably like their counterparts today.

Alarm over the number of train accidents was expressed repeatedly in editorials and newspaper stories through the years, together with a rising chorus of demands that the B&O take measures to prevent them. Double-tracking, the diversion of lower-priority traffic to the less-used old main stem to the north, installation of modern braking and signaling systems, better rails and road bed, and, above all, some control over accidents at grade crossings were all demanded in *Star* editorials. Public concern about the unguarded crossings on Frederick Avenue and Chestnut Street precipitated action by the Maryland General Assembly. An act passed on April 22, 1886 required the B&O to station flagmen there on pain of a $50 fine for each day it failed to do so.

The B&O responded to such complaints with a variety of innovations in safety engineering, though never as promptly and fully as the newspapers demanded. Electrical interlocking systems were installed at Gaithersburg as early as 1890, and the following year the general manager of the railroad reported with satisfaction, "There has been established upon the single-track portion of the Metropolitan Branch, what is believed to be the only single track block system, complete in all detail, at present existing." The block system, as explained in the *Sentinel* in July that year, divided the single-tracked portion of the Metropolitan Branch into a series of 5-mile sections: "At either end of a block are stationed telegraph operators day and night, who watch the movement of trains, note their time of passing, yet no train is allowed to pass into a block unless it is clear that is, until the train that passed last has gone by the station at the farther end of the block or unless it has passed the first station seven minutes before the arrival of the second train." To help deal with the problem of warning vehicular traffic at grade crossings, electric warning bells were installed at Gaithersburg at the end of 1892.

Double-tracking of the line began in 1888 and was substantially completed in 1907. At the same time there was continual upgrading of the line and new automatic signals were installed in 1908. By 1912, block signals and interlocking devices had been installed along the whole route.

For all these safety measures, shocking accidents continued to occur all along the line, especially at grade crossings. Gaithersburg suffered its share of these. Indeed, the heavily traveled grade crossing on Frederick Avenue, long known as "Owen's Crossing," was one of the most dangerous in the state, according to the state roads commission. Though full-time watchmen were employed to guard the crossing, there were no gates to bar road traffic from the path of approaching trains.

One accident in particular roused the community to action. This was the death in 1928 of a popular parish priest, the Reverend John Stanislaus Cuddy, pastor of St. Martin's Catholic Church and St. Rose of Lima Mission. The chamber of commerce backed citizen demands that the crossing be eliminated, and the following June the state roads commission agreed to undertake the work. The present overpass was begun later that year and was completed in December 1930.

In 1957, a government study adopted the rail fans' view that rapid rail service would constitute the best solution to metropolitan Washington's rapidly worsening commuting problem. The B&O demurred. "There isn't a railroad that stays in the commuting business voluntarily, they're forced to," William H. Schmidt of the B&O told a *Sentinel* reporter. "It is a hopelessly unprofitable business. It would take an act of Congress around here [Baltimore] to institute such service."

The Baltimore headquarters for the railroad said it was losing $114,000 a year on the two commuter trains it operated out of Washington and declared that a break-even status was "impossible."

The financial situation steadily worsened. By 1973, the B&O was running an annual deficit of $900,000 on its two commuter lines and the state felt obliged to step in and subsidize the service. In 1974, the Maryland State Department of Transportation paid the railroad some $43,000 monthly, about half the anticipated operating loss. By late 1977, the state estimated that the amount needed to bring service up to an acceptable standard would be $16.9 million. This sum would provide for the purchase and rehabilitation of rail equipment and capital improvements including miscellaneous repairs to the station at Gaithersburg and several other stops along the Metropolitan Branch. Of the total $16.9 million needed, the state proposed that the state and county governments fund $3.4 million and the remaining $13.5 million be provided by a federal grant.

In April 1978, the U.S. Department of Transportation announced a federal grant of $11.8 million to modernize and upgrade service on the Metropolitan Branch and the commuter line from Baltimore. The state and Montgomery and Prince George's Counties were to contribute an additional $3 million as their share of the cost. These sums were expected to double the seating capacity of existing trains and provide for enlarged parking lots and other improvements at various stops, including Gaithersburg. A new station was planned for Metropolitan Grove, on the western outskirts of Gaithersburg.

But the station had not been improved for almost 70 years. It was saved from the wrecker's ball only because the town continued to grow as a source of commuters to Washington, and to the citizens it was a symbol of Gaithersburg.

In 1976, as part of the bicentennial commission's activities, the women's waiting room in the station was refurbished with the aid of volunteer labor and donated materials. Under the layers of old paint, cherry woodwork and window frames were uncovered as well as random-plank pine flooring. The original pot-bellied stove was found and put in the waiting room. A re-dedication ceremony was held in February 1976. The station was a focal point of U.S. bicentennial activities in the city, and after the bicentennial, the Gaithersburg Chamber of Commerce moved into the renovated space.

In fall 1978, the B&O Railroad Station and Freight House were listed on the National Register of Historic Places. This was the first city historic site to have received this honor and at the time one of only 56 stations in the nation so listed. In 1982, the City of Gaithersburg urged Chessie Systems, Inc. (now CSX) to repair and maintain the station and freight house. CSX responded that the required maintenance would be too expensive and suggested demolition as an alternative. On December 20, 1984, the matter was settled. The city's elected officials authorized the purchase of the endangered buildings and site for $525,000.

Community support for this unprecedented public acquisition was overwhelming. A Maryland legislative bill sponsored by the state delegates granted $300,000 toward the total cost of restoration of the buildings, and the city appropriated Capital Improvement Project

Chessie Systems's William Howes and Jack Griffith present a plate to Gaithersburg mayor B. Daniel Walder on May 6, 1978.

funds. The Maryland Historical Trust also provided grant funds. The renovated station complex was dedicated at the 1988 Olde Towne Day opening ceremony. It continues to serve the public as an icon of Gaithersburg, as an attraction for train watchers, as a breakfast and lunch spot in the coffee shop, and as an indoor and outdoor museum of railroading and Gaithersburg at the Gaithersburg Community Museum in the Freight House.

So the railroad line that put Gaithersburg on the map remains an important element in the city and in the area's total transportation system as surface roads become more and more clogged. As far as Gaithersburg and other towns in the mid-county region are concerned, the coming of the railroad was the most important development of the nineteenth and early twentieth centuries, and it is almost solely due to the vision, determination, and unflagging effort of Francis Cassatt Clopper that the Metropolitan Branch of the B&O was called into being and routed through this city.

Locomotive no. 14 from the Buffalo & Gauley line is on display beside the Gaithersburg station.

8. Gaithersburg Incorporates

The railroad spurred the village to prepare for a bigger and better future, but it had a long way to go. Historian T.H.S. Boyd wrote about the newly formed town in his 1879 *History of Montgomery County, Maryland*: "This place was incorporated by the last Legislature and is rapidly improving." He listed two churches, a town hall, and a school as public facilities. The population was recorded as 200.

Governor John Lee Carroll signed an act incorporating the town of Gaithersburg on April 5, 1878. But the charter was far more than a formality; it was the start of Gaithersburg as a true community of citizens with power to make laws, pledge and borrow money, and improve safety and the surroundings. Since 1878 the town has had three forms of government: a board of commissioners from 1878 to 1898, a mayor and council from 1898 to 1962, and a council and manager since 1962. Each was adopted to accommodate specific circumstances and goals.

The 1878 charter established Gaithersburg's first legal government, but it is unlikely that it was actually the village's first effort at government. When people live in close proximity problems arise, and it becomes necessary to organize and attempt to solve those problems. In the eighteenth and nineteenth centuries, wells were used for drinking water, privies were used for sanitary facilities, and it was routine to keep livestock for food and transportation. All of these were potential nuisances and hazards. Common problems were handled on a personal basis, or if enough people were affected, by an ad hoc committee. These committees would convene as needed and disband upon resolution. This was probably the practice in the village before its incorporation, since the committee form survived in the slightly more sophisticated elected board of commissioners, which also met only when "necessary."

No records survive from these informal meetings. A local story relates that the first recorded town meeting occurred in 1850 at the Buriss Blacksmith Shop on Frederick Avenue. In 1850, the greater Gaithersburg area numbered about 225 persons, certainly enough to warrant an occasional meeting about roads, schools, and other common interests.

Gaithersburg wanted to become the new county seat. For a time, this was the town's ultimate ambition. Although a number of citizens were involved in this scheme, we are given only one name, James B. Gaither. According to his obituary on February 27, 1885 in the *Sentinel*, "For years he has been endeavoring to educate and stimulate public

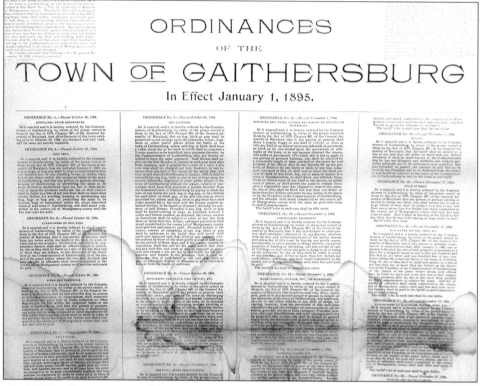

An 1895 ordinance is one of the earliest in the city archives.

sentiment in the direction of the removal of the Court House. However impractical the idea, it showed at least a commendable enterprise on his part."

Rockville was unimpressed by this proposal and a rivalry soon blossomed between the two towns. In the winter of 1881, this took the form of "Sleighing Carnivals," which consisted of up to 120 sleighs driven by costumed citizens preceded by a brass band. The sleighing party paraded the streets of their own and the neighboring rival town. In one episode, the "enterprising village of Gaithersburg . . . brought with them a miniature court house which they very properly carried back as we have a much larger one of our own, which is likely to remain here for many years to come." Rockville repaid the compliment by organizing its own carnival "and took with it a representative Court House, which the prominent citizens of the latter [Gaithersburg] claim properly, belongs there on the grounds of central position."

Moving the courthouse would have taken more than central position and good rail connections to accomplish, however. It required political influence. It may be coincidence, but the town was almost aggressively political from 1880 to 1904 and less active, or at least less successful, after 1904 when the chances for such a move were beyond hope.

But prior to 1878 all dreams seemed attainable, and the town made preparations accordingly. Even before the chartering, a building and loan association had been formed.

The Gaithersburg Mutual Building Association was incorporated March 19, 1877, more than a full year before the town's officially incorporated status. The officers were John T. DeSellum, T.J. Owen, Edmund L. Amiss, Henry C. Ward, Elisha Etchison, Zachariah A. Briggs, and Somerset O. Jones.

This was an interesting mix of old and new families. Ward began his business enterprise in town about 1864. Briggs was the son of Samuel S. Briggs, a large landowner in the area. DeSellum owned most of the land bounded by the present Summit Avenue and the B&O tracks, and all of Summit Hall Farm.

Amiss, the schoolmaster, and Dr. Etchison had arrived in the middle 1870s, as had T.J. Owen, who moved from Goshen about 1874 and opened a store. Jones was a prominent Laytonsville man who served in the general assembly.

Merchants also saw opportunity in the expanding population and they soon became Gaithersburg's early leaders. Thus, led by the Ward, Fulks, Crawford, Owen, Burriss, and Gloyd families, the town built a substantial commercial and industrial base that carried it through the war and depression years.

After incorporation, other merchants and tradesmen came and profited. John A. Belt is listed as holding a liquor license at his store in Beallsville in 1878 but shortly thereafter appears in Gaithersburg. He prospered and served as a town official. John Nicholls's harness business illustrates the lure of railroad, central position, and access roads. In 1878, according to G.W. Hopkins's *Atlas of Montgomery County*, Nicholls was located in the depot area of Germantown and already had rail service. However, there was another harnessmaker in Germantown and the area was not as promising a trade center as Gaithersburg. Nicholls became the first tenant of Diamond Hall in 1874 and remained there throughout his career. The 1894 map shows him as owner of several large lots in the East Diamond area.

THE CHARTER OF 1878

Luckily, the *Sentinel* took an interest in its neighbors' activities. The only information on the incorporation committee is from the paper, including this article from February 22, 1878:

> A meeting of the citizens of Gaithersburg and vicinity was held at Diamond Hall, on the 13th, to take into consideration the expediency of incorporating the village. About a hundred persons were present. The meeting was called to order and T.J. Owen was elected chairman and Dr. E.C. Etchison secretary. The object of the meeting was fully explained, and after some discussion by Messrs. DeSellum, Crawford, Gaither and Owen, it was decided by a resolution of R.G. Dorsey that a committee of three be appointed by the chair to have the bounds surveyed to obtain a plat and get up a petition to the Legislature, and urge our members to have the same passed. The citizens of the village are very enthusiastic over the improvements made in the last year, and are willing and anxious to make some sacrifices, if necessary, to speed it in its happy progress.

The incorporation petition was prepared and sent to the general assembly. It was endorsed by the *Sentinel* on March 22:

> We think our representatives in the Legislature should comply with the wishes of the people of Gaithersburg and have passed an act incorporating them into a municipality. And not alone because its citizens desire it, but because the interests of the County would be greatly enhanced by it. We suppose their object in desiring incorporation is to adorn, beautify and substantially improve their rapidly growing town. To open new streets, to pave sidewalks, to plant out shade trees and accomplish many other things similar to those which have made Rockville the beautiful and attractive village it is. Nothing more readily allures visitors and those who are looking for a permanent home to a neighborhood than near, pretty, inviting villages, and Gaithersburg is peculiarly situated to be of more than ordinary attraction, for its streets and its houses are visible from the railroad where hundreds of strangers pass every day. A great many farmers have migrated from the West here, and the more attractive our county the more will come. Again we say, grant them the law and let them improve their town.

The law was passed, and for the first 20 years of its government, Gaithersburg was a body corporate registered in the name of "The Commissioners of Gaithersburg." Its 28-section charter was approved by the Maryland state legislature and signed by the governor. The government consisted of a five-member commission that had all power for conduct of local affairs. The member receiving the highest number of votes was the president. Commissioners were required to be substantial citizens and reside within corporate limits for at least six months. Except for the president, they received no pay. The president was vested with the power of a justice of the peace in all criminal cases involving the corporation and could receive fees.

The first town election was reported by the *Sentinel* on April 26, 1878:

> Gaithersburg is beginning to "brace up" for its future greatness. A meeting was held this week to arrange all preliminaries for the election of town officers, which comes off on the first Monday in May. Reports advise us that "excitement prevails and that candidates are as numerous as citizens."

Seven candidates ran: T.J. Owen, H.C. Ward, J.B. Gaither, W.A. Gloyd, S.S. Gloyd Jr., R.A. Burriss, and C.W. Crawford. Crawford, Ward, Burriss, and W.A. Gloyd were elected and a run-off election was held the following Monday to break a tie vote, with J.B. Gaither the winner over Samuel S. Gloyd Jr.

Minutes of the proceedings were handwritten in bound books and were available for public inspection. However, the minutes were often incomplete. Members present were often not listed, and at times, voting was by secret ballot. Important details often went unrecorded, such as the first 16 ordinances passed on June 29, 1878. A bailiff, John A. Burriss, brother of Commissioner Reuben Burriss, was appointed to enforce the ordinances, collect taxes and fines, attend all commission meetings, and preserve the

Crews reconstruct Diamond Avenue in the 1960s.

peace. He received an additional salary of $15 per year over his fees for patrolling the streets every Saturday night from 7:00 to 11:00 p.m.

The primary business of the first government was roads and sidewalks. Existing roads were named Frederick Avenue, Diamond Avenue, Park Avenue (West Diamond), and Chestnut Street. Intersections were piked with stone and an oak plank sidewalk was built on the west side of Frederick Avenue.

As the 1880s progressed, prospects for gaining the new courthouse died. By 1890, Gaithersburg had already experienced dissension and had outgrown its simple commission government. The problems had begun early and evidently reflected the rivalries and dissent in the town. In 1879, T.J. Owen challenged the May election. The board called a meeting on May 19 at Crawford and Etchison's Drugstore to hear Owen's grievances, "caused as he, the sd. T.J. Owen claimed on account of the illegality of an election for Town Commissioners held the 5th day of May, 1879, in which the sd. T. Owen was a candidate."

After much discussion on the subject, the board decided that it had no jurisdiction in the case. On May 4, 1880, John W. Owen protested, this time as to the qualifications of the commissioners elected, claiming the recent election to be fraudulent. After more discussion, the board adjourned. Before the objection the new commission, H.C. Ward, R.A. Burriss, E.C. Etchison, and M.S. Benton, took the oath of office. James B. Gaither, the fifth elected commissioner, was not present. The board finally met "for the purpose of hearing further Mr. John W. Owen's protest." Again, there was no action. "Mr. John W. Owen having been notified at a late hour that the Board was ready for action failed to come whereupon the old Board of Commissioners dismissed the case and Mr. H.C. Ward, the new President took the chair."

Gaithersburg's corporate limits have expanded to include the area around Route 355 and the I-270 interchange, as pictured in 1960.

After this, a petition from the citizens praising the certain improvements at different points in the upper village was read before the board and ordered filed. The new board's problems continued at the next meeting. Another petition signed by S.S. Gloyd, T.J. Owen, and other taxpayers asking for a reduction in taxes was read and ordered filed. The levy for 1880–1881 was set at one-tenth of 1 percent, one-half the 1878 rate. James B. Gaither offered a motion "to bind each member over to secrecy so far as the proceedings of sd. board were concerned," but the motion lost.

The division within the town became public knowledge via the *Sentinel's* May 9, 1884 account of the election:

> The election for five commissioners of Gaithersburg, this county, was held on Monday last. There were seven candidates. Giles Easton received 30 votes, N.E. Selby 14, C.F. Linthicum 45, C.F. Hogan 26, Geo. Meem 37, S.S. Gloyd 43, C.F. Duvall 27. Easton, Linthicum, Meem, Gloyd, and Duvall were the successful candidates and constitute the Board. The interest in the election was the division between up-town and low-town struggling for the election of representatives in the Board of Commissioners to manage the town affairs. Low-town gained the day with much feeling at the result, for the first time for five years.

In 1888, the town and its government experienced some legal changes. Chapter 541 of the Laws of Maryland expanded the area of the town south of the railroad to just past

Summit Avenue, annexed other parcels, and provided a two-year term of office for elected officials rather than one. Also in 1888, Thomas B. Brookes appeared before the commissioners requesting the opening of three new roads connecting his property to Diamond and Frederick Avenues. This was approved several months later—the roads were named Brookes, Russell, and Park Avenues—and the ground was subdivided. The new boundaries of the town were surveyed, platted, and entered at the county surveyor's office in 1894.

By 1890, those who had considered the town a personal enterprise had either died or sensed that boom-town profits were not going to appear overnight. It was time to dig in and prepare for the long haul, but with a more democratic spirit. The commission form allowed little citizen representation or real participation. Redress and special procedures were not clearly defined. The president of the commission served as justice of the peace as far as city business was concerned, which was not comforting to alleged offenders. Officials were frequently paid for various jobs after inadequate or no bid procedures. It was time for a change, and a new charter for the town was soon submitted to the general assembly.

THE MAYOR AND COUNCIL CHARTER OF 1898

The second charter was granted by the general assembly on April 9, 1898 and signed by Governor Lloyd Lownces. It established a corporate body known as "The Town of Gaithersburg" as the legal successor to the Commissioners of Gaithersburg. In general, it defined the specific powers of the council in far greater detail and provided for a mayor. Methods of grievance, redress, and appeal were included. The functioning of the government was regulated and a certain amount of disclosure and accountability was assured. The charter itself grew from six handwritten sheets containing 28 brief sections to 15 printed pages and 36 sections.

A mayor and four councilmen were elected to replace the five commissioners. The council was to meet in a "suitable public space designated as a regular place of meeting" and meet as often as necessary, but not less than once every three months. The needed election challenge and appeals procedures were outlined. The powers of the council were enumerated at great length while not unduly restricting it. But by far the longest additions were the sections that defined the processes of tax assessment, appeal, notice, procedures of tax sales, and redemption rights. These sections occupy four-and-a-half pages and were probably prompted by the default of Brookes and Russell.

Other reform measures were added. Ordinances were to be adopted by a yea or nay vote and the names and votes were to be recorded in the minutes. The council was required to keep and annually publish or post a financial statement of the corporation and "other matters connected with the government and regulations of the town affairs as they may deem necessary and proper." Provisions to guarantee fair compensation for private property taken for public use and for condemnation procedures and appeal appeared. Work estimated to cost more than $200 required bids solicited by notice and publication.

Carlisle Hall was selected as the permanent meeting place and leased for $20 per year. Later, the Masonic Hall was used until the firehouse on East Diamond and Russell

Avenues was built for both town offices and the fire department before the purchase of the present City Hall. The mayor-council form of government prevailed through four more charters until 1962. It was accompanied by a comfortable ratio of commercial economic base to citizens needing services.

The first election under the new charter of Gaithersburg, held the first Monday night in June 1898, resulted in the election of a new player as mayor. George W. Meem won the mayoral office by three votes in a warm contest with ex-councilman R. Dorsey Trundle. New faces also appeared on the council, which was composed of Thomas I. Fulks, James T. English, David G. Carlisle, and Richard H. Miles. According to the *Sentinel*, all were considered in favor of the "needed reforms" promised in the new town charter and were elected for two years.

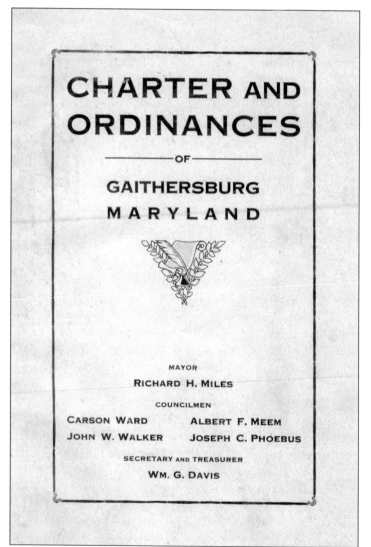

A 1914–1915 ordinance book depicts the town's rules and regulations.

9. THE TWENTIETH CENTURY

A look at the 1900 census gives us a glimpse of Gaithersburg's progress in its first 22 years of incorporation. It grew remarkably in percentages but not in total numbers. The town started with 200 residents in 1878, but it was still a small town. In 1900, there were 114 households and a total of 547 residents: 289 women and 258 men. The census indicates that about half of these families rented their homes and six families in the town lived on farms. Households often included extended families: servants, employees, and boarders, and often single, elderly persons such as Frances Roome, Gaithersburg's oldest resident in 1900. She was born in 1812.

George Waters, who was born and raised at 21 Brookes Avenue, recalled those days:

> There was a man, aptly named Harry Smith, who was our Blacksmith. His place of business was located on Diamond Avenue near the First National Bank between the Carlisle Mortuary with the furniture store on its right side and the Miller Livery Stable on its left. As I remember, he lived just outside town at the end of Summit Avenue North, where Goshen Road begins.
>
> Back then, it was good business with no local competition. Horses were necessary for productive farming as well as for transportation and needed horseshoes to protect their feet. Mr. Smith had to be a muscular and careful man to make and apply these shoes. When his customers were being fitted, they had to stand on only three legs. The fourth one rested on Mr. Smith's lap. In order to protect himself, Mr. Smith wore a heavy leather apron. The shoe was made of iron and came in a variety of shades, which indicated sizes. In order to make the shoe fit properly, he had to place the shoe in his forge and hammer it into exact shape and size while red hot. It was then put into a tub of water to cool it down before nailing it on the hoof. This procedure was carried out on all four hoofs.
>
> It was a fascinating experience for me to witness this customized shoe fitting and the precise methods of putting nails into the hooves of those helpful horses. Those good shoes helped the horses to give long service.

Professionals living in Gaithersburg at the time included an architect, a banker, three lawyers, and six merchants. The town's dentist, three physicians, four nurses, and druggist were available to take care of the sick. Six schoolteachers also made their home in

These 1930 members of the Gaithersburg–Washington Grove Fire Department are preparing for the Labor Day parade. (Courtesy of Merle T. Jacobs.)

Gaithersburg. In 1900, just as today, Gaithersburg residents worked for the federal government, commuting to work by train. They worked for agencies such as the Treasury Department, War Department, Navy Department, Post Office Department, and the Pension Office.

Gaithersburg women were employed as nurses, seamstresses, dressmakers, schoolteachers, and stenographers. Mrs. Eytinse Hinkley, however, a 67-year-old widow, was recorded as a farmer. Hinkley's nursery and truck garden was located on North Frederick Avenue west of the present Asbury Village property.

George Waters's mother, Nettie, managed the Forest Oak Hotel on Diamond Avenue in the 1920s. She also managed a house and family. Everyone had chores, and George remembered his time tending the chickens:

> Back in these early years, 1910 to 1925, town residents had backyard chicken coops and fowl were part of our country living experience. As a boy, my family assignment was to care for the chickens we had in our backyard at 21 Brookes Avenue. It was my mother Nettie Waters' preference to raise the hearty flock known as Plymouth Rock which she considered the best. We had a large backyard with lots of space for them to range as well as a spacious hen house. It was my job to keep their roosting home clean and comfortable for their egg

production. Each day I gathered brown eggs from the nests, which provided our family and guests with delicious fresh food. Our chicks, the offspring of the Plymouth mothers, became another source of fine meals. While our hens were the real producers, hatching their eggs in their comfortable nests provided young ones for consumption. All during life in their backyard habitat, the young birds seemed to like what they had going for them, but eventually lost their heads.

In 1900, we can see hints of the change and growth to come. At the turn of the century both farmers and government employees called Gaithersburg home. Doctors, teachers, and other professionals were sufficient in number to take care of the town's needs and the number of merchants, builders, and craftsmen reflect the fact that the town was prosperous and growing.

The social order changed as well with new citizens and a new form of government. A 1912 social survey of the county concluded that in Clarksburg, Barnesville, Poolesville, and Laytonsville, "socially there is little or no opportunity of passing from one class to another." But in Gaithersburg, "there are three social standards, in general conforming to the three groups of farm-owners, tenants, and laborers. These lines are not hard and fast, and are easily stepped over; one great reason for this is that for 15 or 20 years most of the young people have belonged to the so-called 'middle-class.' There are only two economic standards, as there is practically no difference between owner and tenant in this respect." The study concluded that un-crossable social lines existed in communities where "the entire community seldom if ever acts as a unit."

So Gaithersburg was a mobile society. This was largely due to its position as a thriving agricultural trade center. It was recognized as a primary shipping and receiving point for the surrounding agricultural areas. Since double-tracking of the Metropolitan Branch ended between Gaithersburg and Germantown, intensive use also ended at Gaithersburg. This is reflected in the condition of the feeder roads. Three of Gaithersburg's feeders were classed as among the 14 best market roads in the county.

Thus the town became self-sufficient. It established its own industrial sector. The Gaithersburg Milling and Manufacturing Company had been founded in 1891 and on September 19, 1917, Thomas and Company requested permits for a flour mill, grain elevator, fertilizer mixing plant, and a canning factory in Gaithersburg. Many smaller farm and domestic suppliers were already present.

The charter that passed on April 10, 1914 updated the powers of the mayor and council, recognizing such recent innovations as electricity, indoor plumbing, and automobiles. It inaugurated the staggered four-year term for council members, while preserving the two-year office of mayor. The council was now required to meet not less than once a month. The mayor and council were authorized to borrow up to $5,000 on the credit of the town for street and sidewalk improvements. A budget deficit had been carried for the first time in 1901, and D.G. Carlisle was delegated by the council to borrow $250 to cover the shortage. This was unusual, however; the town was required to maintain a balanced budget. Non-resident taxpayers were allowed to vote for the first time and gambling was forbidden. The tax assessment and sale procedures were continued from 1906.

The mayor and council revised and updated the ordinances of the town in 1915. These included the familiar ones dealing with sanitation, livestock in town, dogs at large, vagrants, and other public nuisances. Fear of epidemic diseases prompted the denial of a public funeral for any person dying of a contagious disease, and a quarantine of the household for 15 days. Automobiles were dealt with at length in ordinance no. 6. Their maximum legal speed was fixed at 12 miles per hour and they were to pull over and stop when meeting an animal that might become frightened.

A newly revised charter was published in booklet form in 1929 with current ordinances in a second section. Although the town had received sewage and water service in 1924, many of the ordinances still dealt with privies, cesspools, and other sanitary facilities as many residents did not want to pay connection fees to hook into the lines. Typhoid and other health problems continued to plague the town. Cleanliness was a necessity, and often the council was requested to inspect privies. The mayor, as chief executive, was generally assigned this chore. Despite all these efforts, disease still took a toll. On September 17, 1931, a letter was sent to Dr. Pratt, the county health officer, "in regard to the typhoid epidemic in Gaithersburg." The town asked, "What is the cause, and what authority [do] the mayor and council have to remedy this condition in future?"

On March 6, 1933, the first zoning ordinance was adopted. Irving C. Root of Silver Spring was appointed city planner at a salary of $150, and the zoning committee consisted of H.H. Ramsdell, H.S. Kingsley, Bates Etchison, Thomas Waters, and William D. Barnett. Norman Jacobs served in place of Waters when the committee became the new board of zoning appeals.

By 1944, the skeleton of today's departmental government existed in committee form. The most active was the street improvement committee. The building code committee was instigated on November 1, 1944, partly at the suggestion of the Neighborhood Garden Club. On June 5, the committee recommended that the Building Code of Montgomery County be adopted as the official Gaithersburg code. At the same meeting the recreation council committee representative reported that "recreation nights were well attended." A catch basin (storm sewers) committee was acting in December 1945. Other committees were convened as circumstances merited.

As late as 1952 the town was still personally administered by the elected representatives. This included both major decisions and minor details. On May 5, 1952, for example, the agenda included reports from the street improvement committee, revising zoning committee, violation of fire code committee, "sign at S.F. Smith Garage committee," and the "committee for reducing the porch at Byrne Store." Next came the town attorney's opinion on the status of a pending lawsuit and Mayor Perry's report that the guy-wire on Hutton had been reset. Councilman Fox was appointed to investigate a complaint that a local welder's windows were unshielded and that "children looking in the window could be injured." Another citizen complained that chickens were ruining her strawberry bed, and a request for a parking regulation exception was read. Three months later the council passed an ordinance banning poultry at large within the corporate limits, thus presumably saving the strawberry bed.

The 1950s were a difficult time for the town, which was turning into a city while many residents still clung to small-town ways. For example, in 1950, placards stating "No Hog

Raising in Corporate Limits" were ordered posted in Deer Park. Also known as "Paradise," Deer Park was annexed in 1947 along with property on the west side of Frederick Avenue. On May 3, 1954, a permit for 28 dwellings on Tulip Drive in Deer Park was granted despite the protests of owners on Peony and Hutton that the $7,600 one-bedroom models with expandable carport would decrease existing property values.

In 1954 and 1955, electric and gas codes were adopted. Even more expansion was on the horizon and it became obvious that some major changes would have to be made. Other events forced a new look at the government and its goals in the late 1950s. In 1957, the section of the Annotated Code of Maryland dealing with planning presented a model charter for municipalities. Limitations and procedures were defined, but according to the new code as long as a municipality was in compliance, no legislative approval was necessary for rechartering.

REGIONAL PLANNING AND COUNCIL-MANAGER GOVERNMENT

The 1958 charter, based on the 1957 Maryland model, was the longest at 98 sections with further subdivisions. Nevertheless, even without the state action, a change would have been necessary in the next few years. Both the Montgomery County and the Washington metropolitan area planners were formulating long-term plans that affected Gaithersburg

The Polkadot Drive In occupied the original office of the Diamond Milling Company.

111

in every way, especially in transportation, utilities, and land use. It was no longer possible or even desirable for the town to remain an independent fiefdom in the midst of a larger territory. In the words of one writer of the time, it would have ended up being "the hole in the doughnut." Thus began the era of regional planning.

The new charter provided for all sorts of licensing, regulations, and enforcement. It provided the right to establish, operate, and maintain a police force; to exercise the powers of planning and zoning conferred upon municipal corporations generally by the Annotated Code of Maryland; to establish a board of supervisors of the council; to levy and collect taxes in the form of special assessments upon property; and to divide the civil service of the town into unclassified and classified service.

The mayor was the chief executive and administrative head of the government. He was responsible for reporting the condition of municipal affairs including the town's financial state and for preparing and submitting the annual budget. The mayor was elected for a four-year term and received an annual salary, as did the council members, who increased in number from four to five, were elected to four-year terms, and in whom all legislative powers were vested.

As town population and interaction with other jurisdictions increased, the job of chief administrator became too demanding for a part-time mayor. Therefore in 1962, section 20

Mayor Bruce Goldensohn cuts Gaithersburg's 100th birthday cake on April 7, 1978.

of the 1958 charter was amended to provide for the appointment of a salaried town administrator or manager having executive capabilities to handle the day-to-day affairs of the mayor and council.

The manager received the powers formerly held by the mayor: the role as head administrator and executive officer, the responsibility to appoint personnel and heads of departments, the duty to report on municipal affairs and make recommendations, and the complete supervision of the financial aspects of government. A majority vote of the council is required to appoint or remove the city manager.

Under this form of government the mayor is still the official head of the city for ceremonial purposes with responsibilities as set forth in the charter. The mayor, although a non-voting member, is president of the council with the power to veto finances and make appointments to city boards, commissions, and committees, subject to confirmation by the council. Legislative powers are vested in a five-member council whose elected offices are on staggered four-year terms. Representative of the citizens, the council is responsible for the overall operation of the government. It appoints the city manager, adopts an annual budget, enacts city laws, levies taxes, and enters into contracts and agreements.

After the council-manager form of government was instituted, programs became departmentalized under finance, planning, public works, licenses and inspections, parks and recreation, police, and general government. Heads of these departments and other employees are hired by the city manager or a designee.

The first town administrator was Patrick Gaffigan who was appointed in June 1963 and resigned in November 1964. William Vose was appointed in March 1965 and resigned in March 1968. Sanford Daily was appointed June 1968 and retired February 1995. David Humpton was appointed that same month and is the current city manager.

Gaithersburg is a fiscally responsible city that has not incurred any bond debts since 1963. It maintains a pay-as-you-go financial philosophy that allows it to enjoy a prosperous economic status. The tax rate has not changed in more than 38 years, making Gaithersburg an attractive place to live, work, learn, and play.

There is a close relationship between the citizens of Gaithersburg and the elected officials that run the government. The importance of this relationship is seen at the mayor and city council meetings during the "public appearances" portion when citizens bring their concerns and issues to their elected officials. The lines of communication are open in the community, which facilitates the ability for the government to work for the people.

In 1996, mayor and city council meetings began airing live on the city's cable television station. Two years later the channel expanded to include the airing of work sessions, and then planning commission meetings in 2000. In the winter of 2001, Gaithersburg was the first city in the state to provide streaming video of these live meetings and other cable programs on the city's website.

The charter of 1958 brought another change to the town. It had outgrown its small offices at the fire station and purchased an elegant house on Summit Avenue to be used as a civic center and town hall. Today, the renovated 1895 building is known as the Sanford Daily Municipal Center, or more commonly Gaithersburg City Hall.

THE NATIONAL INSTITUTE OF STANDARDS AND TECHNOLOGY

In 1901, just two years after Edwin Smith set up his small observatory in Gaithersburg under the direction of the U.S. Coast and Geodetic Survey (CGS), 11 men moved into the CGS offices in downtown Washington. They were the entire staff of the National Bureau of Standards (NBS), now the National Institute of Standards and Technology (NIST), which was created by an act of Congress on March 3, 1901. The act provided that:

> The functions of the bureau shall consist in the custody of the standards; the comparison of the standards used in scientific investigations, engineering, manufacturing commerce, and educational institutions with the standards adopted or recognized by the Government; the construction, when necessary, of standards, their multiples and subdivisions; the testing and calibration of standard measuring apparatus; the solution of problems which arise in connection with standards; the determination of physical constants and the properties of materials, when such data are of great importance to scientific or manufacturing interests and are not to be obtained of sufficient accuracy elsewhere.

These tasks were too large to be long contained in the back rooms of the CGS, and the first building at Connecticut Avenue and Van Ness Street was completed in 1904. By the late 1950s, the District of Columbia campus was proving too confining and the urban environment affected sensitive experiments. These developments coincided with the administration's efforts to decentralize Washington's federal facilities to reduce its vulnerability to nuclear attack. First, the NBS divisions concerned with electromagnetics, time and frequency, cryogenics and quantum physics were moved to Boulder, Colorado, but almost half of those employees scheduled for the move resigned.

Congress approved the decision to relocate the main NBS campus, but placed two limitations upon the selection of the new site: "It must be at least 20 miles from the center of Washington, and it could not be in the Washington-Baltimore corridor."

Bureau management imposed several other limitations on the selection of the new location. It had to consist of at least 400 acres and be relatively level and reasonably high, have good access by highway, and be convenient to the homes of most NBS scientists.

The purchase of 555 acres in Gaithersburg in 1957 resolved most of the Bureau's difficulties, although when Robert S. Walleigh was planning the move many called it "Walleigh's Falleigh." The John B. Diamond farm constituted the bulk of the site in Gaithersburg and the old Briggs property along Muddy Branch Road provided much of the remainder. The site has outstanding accessibility by road, being next to Interstate 270 and between Maryland Route 124 and Muddy Branch Road, and it was also close to a railroad.

The site contains adequate land for further construction and isolated areas for sensitive buildings such as the hazard laboratory and reactor buildings. In addition, the rural location removes the Bureau's work from a variety of mechanical, electrical, and atmospheric disturbances present in a city and reduces the effects of these factors on precise scientific measurements. A further advantage of such a location is that scientific experiments can be conducted with a minimum of interference to community life. It was far enough from the District to escape a possible nuclear strike, but it was close enough that employees could commute from their existing homes. The land was available for an estimated $750,000.

In advance of the relocation, NBS officials began working with the mayor of Gaithersburg, the Montgomery County Council, the Maryland National Capital Park and Planning Commission, and other authorities. The community was made aware of NBS's special needs to be protected against avoidable mechanical, electrical, and atmospheric disturbances. A spin-off from this collaboration was the development of industrial park zoning concepts.

Groundbreaking for the first Bureau of Standards building in Gaithersburg took place on June 14, 1961, and formal dedication ceremonies were held on November 15, 1966. Tradition was not forgotten. With great care an apple tree was brought from England. It was said to be a direct descendant of the tree under which Sir Isaac Newton was sitting when, according to legend, he discovered the law of gravity. It was nurtured to a full-sized tree and planted on the grounds. The old wrought-iron gates from the Connecticut and Van Ness Campus were brought out and placed at the entrance to the new facility.

The decision to relocate to Gaithersburg was nearly overwhelming in its effect on the town. Realizing that growth would be rapid, the town changed to a city manager form of government so that a full-time professional could help guide Gaithersburg's progress.

An old NBS sign of the 1960s marks the way along I-270 when it was only four lanes.

The new town administrator William O. Vose wrote, "The year 1966 will long be remembered as the year in which the Town became known as the 'Science Capital of the United States.' " The opening of the huge National Bureau of Standards complex was largely responsible for this new designation for Gaithersburg, which is probably the only community in the United States of 8,000 people that can boast 4,000 science-oriented jobs.

In 1966, the Kettler Brothers were planning construction of homes in Montgomery Village to house all the new workers. Gaithersburg opened its first two shopping centers that year, Gaithersburg Square and the Duvall Shopping Center, both in anticipation of growth and contributing to that growth.

The Federal Systems Division of IBM opened its doors in Gaithersburg in 1966. The National Geographic Society broke ground in that year also. Communications Satellite Corporation purchased a site a little to the north of the city. By 1978, the NBS was Gaithersburg's largest employer and other science-related industries have continued to locate in or near Gaithersburg. Since the arrival of the NBS, the population of Gaithersburg grew from 8,000 to 45,793.

In 1988, as a result of the Omnibus Trade and Competitiveness Act, the National Bureau of Standards formally became the National Institute of Standards and Technology. Today, the NIST promotes economic growth in the United States by working with industry to develop and apply technology, measurements, and standards through technology-based tools.

Kentlands

The Tschiffely-Kent property has been a landmark along Darnestown Road for more than 100 years. The mansion there was built in 1900 by Frederick A. Tschiffely Jr. of Washington. An article in the June 15, 1900 *Sentinel* reported that he had started construction of a fine brick residence, "The Wheatlands," on his farm near Quince Orchard for a cost of $10,000.

When Tschiffely's father came to Montgomery County he was 34 years old and the owner of a successful large drug wholesale business in the District of Columbia. In 1852, he purchased more than 200 acres along Darnestown Road near the village of Gaithersburg from the Joseph Clagett heirs for a country estate and summer retreat.

Tschiffely became a prosperous farmer who continued to acquire parcels surrounding his new farm. He took an active role in the religious, social, and economic development of the community and donated property for a new school and to the Presbyterian Church. At the time of his death, he had amassed the farm and another 242 acres that were inherited by Frederick Jr. after his mother died in 1900.

Frederick Tschiffely Jr. was a pharmacist who owned a wholesale drugstore business at 475 Pennsylvania Avenue Northwest in the District of Columbia. He and his wife, Dolly Brown, and their eight children lived at the estate in Montgomery County. Upton Burris, the overseer, drove Tschiffely via horse and buggy to and from the train station for his daily commute to Washington.

Tschiffely kept pharmaceuticals at his home and residents of the county would come to him for prescriptions. Many visitors referred to the estate as the "The Bricks" because of the heavy use of brick in the main house, overseer's house, gate house, carriage house, barn, chicken house, and numerous other outbuildings.

The farm produced wheat and corn as major crops. In later years, actual farming decreased and most of the land was kept in pasture for cows, horses, and sheep. Tschiffely also raised racehorses and, in 1911, allowed Montgomery County to operate the quarry on the farm that mined rocks to build county roads.

The *Klinge Real Estate Atlas* of 1917 showed the Tschiffely holdings to be 648 acres. Like his father, Frederick Jr. continued to aggressively purchase property until his death in 1931 at age 91. The August 31 *Sentinel* carried his obituary: "Years ago he acquired the family farm, Wheatlands, and added to it from time to time till it is now regarded as one of the county's largest and finest estates." The farm was bequeathed to his two oldest sons and two oldest daughters.

The next generation of Tschiffelys lived closer to Washington and the Darnestown estate began to serve as a summer place that was operated by tenants. The 601.73-acre farm was sold to Otis Beall Kent in 1942, at which time Wheatlands became Kentlands.

Kent was a wealthy attorney who dramatically changed the main house, outbuildings, and the estate property. He enlarged the mansion to display his sizable and valuable collection of Oriental rugs, books, artwork, and jewels. Modern greenhouses were built and the stables were reconstructed to house his private fire engines. He was a strong advocate for the preservation of all wildlife. Ponds and lakes were constructed on the property to provide a habitat and sanctuary for birds and game. Before his death in 1972, Kent agreed to sell some acreage to the National Geographic Society with a strict wildlife

This photograph of Kentlands was taken at the turn of the twentieth century.

protective covenant that prohibited hunting, fishing, or trapping of any bird or animal on or in the lakes or elsewhere on the property.

After Kent's death, Kentlands was bequeathed to his adopted daughter Helene Danger Kent. She lived in the house until the property was acquired by the Great Seneca Limited Partnership in 1988, thus bringing to a close this property's 136 years as a private estate.

The Kentlands community began with a vision of Joseph Alfandre and Co. to create a new nineteenth-century American town on the remaining 352 acres. Following two years of complex and innovative design review and approval under the tutelage of renowned urban planners Andres Duany and Elizabeth Plyter-Zerbek, groundbreaking ceremonies for the neo-traditional town within the corporate limits of Gaithersburg were celebrated on October 27, 1989.

The city and its residents looked forward with great enthusiasm to the preservation and restoration of the Tschiffely historic buildings for public use and the addition of innovative housing units of all types. The retail center supporting commercial uses, an impressive entertainment-oriented Midtown, and the public buildings, including the Kentland Mansion and Arts Barn, offer every resident of Gaithersburg new cultural and civic opportunities equaled by none. Modeled after the Kentlands, the adjoining Lakelands neighborhood also offers a variety of neo-traditional housing and commercial properties.

The "yellow room" at Kentlands served as the Tschiffely family's main parlor at the turn of the twentieth century.

10. City Hall

The large Victorian house was built as the residence of Henry and Rosa Miller on property purchased by Rosa Miller in 1885 from Mary Augusta and William R. Hutton. It was not the first Miller home on the property, however; their first house was the Wells-Robertson House at 1 Wells Avenue, which is also owned by the city and is the site of a highly successful treatment program for homeless and addicted people. A handwritten inscription found on interior timbers of the Wells-Robertson House dates its construction to 1885. City Hall was built ten years later in 1895. The ten-room Victorian Colonial Revival residence was the height of architectural fashion in that year, "being in the most modern style, with such conveniences as steam heat and hot and cold water." Miller was a prosperous man who was a business partner of J. Sprigg Poole, Lee Lipscomb, and Thomas Brooks. His fortunes fell upon hard times and consequently his estate was auctioned in 1910.

In 1913, Edward P. Schwartz of Washington purchased the 5-acre property from the mortgage holder at a public sale. Schwartz was a successful real estate broker in the District of Columbia but he moved his household to Summit Avenue that same summer. It was definitely a gentleman's country estate—the cook had her own cottage in back of the main house and there was a two-car garage, a windmill, and a pump house. On the south side of the house, where the handball practice wall is now, there was a tennis court and games area. The remodeling included bringing electricity to the house, making it the first residence in Gaithersburg to boast this amenity.

Schwartz was an enthusiastic gardener, and he created a formal garden between the house and the railroad tracks. At first it was a traditional rose garden with gravel walks arranged in concentric circles and squares. A spectacular row of red canna lilies ran from the garden down to Summit Avenue, which was still a dirt road, and the entire garden was bordered with cherry trees. In his yard, Schwartz found a fine example of a peony flower, which he took to the Department of Agriculture for identification. They established it as a Madame Costa, showed him how to subdivide the roots to increase his stock, and volunteered that Gaithersburg had an almost ideal climate for peony culture. From this original plant, Schwartz made 35 root cuttings and began to purchase other varieties. Between 1914 and 1923, he imported more than 40,000 plants in 410 varieties from England, Japan, France, Germany, and the Netherlands.

Every spring tourists would come to view the fantastic display of color at the "World Famous Schwartz Peony Garden." The gardeners planted an American flag in red and white peonies and blue irises along what is now Hutton Street. Peonies grown for sale to florists and fanciers covered the property between the house and the railroad tracks. Passengers on the trains would crowd to the windows to see one of the largest peony gardens in the country and even President Woodrow Wilson came to Gaithersburg in 1918 to view the flowers. Another famous regular visitor was Gilbert Grosvenor, president of the National Geographic Society, who made many photographs of the gardens.

After Schwartz died in 1924, his widow continued the care of the gardens. Mrs. Schwartz died in 1941, but her children kept the gardens for another five years and then moved them to a farm on Clopper Road, which is now Seneca Creek State Park. Here a few of the world famous Schwartz peonies still survive.

The house remained a residence for a dozen more years before the town bought the buildings and property for use as a town office building and recreation center in 1958. The conversion combined the living and dining rooms to create the city council chambers for public meetings. The library was remodeled to provide a small kitchen and relaxation area for employees. The larger original kitchen was remodeled into office space, as were all six upstairs bedrooms. In 1963, when the Gaithersburg Department of the Police services was established, a trailer for police and recreation departments was placed in the rear of the building.

Hannah Marie and Irene Schwartz stand with the family dog outside their Summit Avenue home that became City Hall. (Courtesy of Irene Schwartz Emmet.)

In August 1971, more office space was needed. Taking advantage of Mayor Harold Morris's expertise as a builder, the city used him as an advisor and consultant. Public works director Archie McLachlen provided the design, and city employees actually constructed a two-story addition to the building on the side closest to Hutton Street. This provided a new city manager's office and anteroom upstairs and a new reception office downstairs. The vault, a concrete closet with concrete floor, received a new concrete ceiling at this time, too.

In fall 1968, a resolution was adopted giving city status to Gaithersburg and a new seal, symbolic of the research and development in and around Gaithersburg, was approved. In the same year, the mayor and city council took action to recodify the charter and laws of the city. The new fundamental law and constitution became known as the Gaithersburg City Code. An updated city code was issued in 1970, and it is constantly amended.

The council-manager system furnishes more stability and more continuity to the city government. However, it is not as immediate as other forms. Previously, the mayor was the chief executive and all responsibility rested on that office. Dissatisfaction could be registered in the most direct way, by electing another person as mayor. Now voters must elect five council members over a period of six years to implement a complete change in policy, whereas theoretically the replacement of the mayor accomplished this before. But time has shown that the mayor and council must work together to be effective, and Gaithersburg citizens have not wanted professional elected governmental officials. It has always preferred volunteers who are involved with the city in a variety of ways and whose income does not depend upon a city salary.

As Gaithersburg's population grew from 3,487 in 1960 to 26,420 in 1980, elected officials realized the city needed more staff and community services and commissioned an architect to design an addition and renovation of City Hall in 1979. On June 9, 1986, a groundbreaking ceremony for the office addition was held with Mayor Bohrer and the city council, as well as past mayors Bruce Goldensohn, Susan Nicholson, and Milton Walker, in attendance. City staff moved into the new addition in January 1988, and it was dedicated during Olde Towne Day ceremonies on September 17, 1989. Irving T. Fulks was honored as Citizen of the Year on the restored porch of City Hall. Finishing touches to the original building were completed in November and the council met in the new chambers on December 4, 1989.

In 1994, the planning department and the building and code department were consolidated on the first floor to offer visitors convenient, one-stop shopping at City Hall. The police department also moved from the basement to the city's newly acquired building at 5 Cedar Avenue. In February 1995, City Hall was renamed Sanford Daily Municipal Center in honor of city manager Daily who retired after 27 years of service.

CITY DEPARTMENTS

Gaithersburg city government has seven departments: the office of the city manager; police; parks, recreation, and culture; planning and code administration; finance and administration; information technology; and public works, park maintenance, and engineering.

OFFICE OF THE CITY MANAGER

The city manager directs and coordinates the general administration of the city government, which includes preparation of the annual budget. The mission of the office of the city manager is to implement the policies set forth by the mayor and council; the city manager coordinates the enforcement and execution of all laws and ordinances of the city.

The office of the city manager also includes mayoral and council services, economic development, environmental affairs, public information and marketing (cable television and a website that contains more than 2,000 pages of information and streams live video of the city's Channel 13), and human resources and human services. This department provides management and administrative support for all of the city departments.

Each year this department facilitates the mayor and council's strategic planning process in which new goals and priorities are set by developing strategic directions. These directions relate to the city's mission, vision, and guiding principles. The office of the city manager prepares updated reports concerning progress made with each strategic direction. These directions are used to guide budget preparation, which the city manager begins in the new year. During the budget preparation process, a public meeting is held to hear concerns and gain input from citizens. The budget process then continues under the direction of the city manager until it is approved by the mayor and council each June.

GAITHERSBURG POLICE DEPARTMENT

Gaithersburg had several forms of local justice before it established a formal police department in 1963. At first, there was a bailiff and a justice of the peace. Prior to 1963, the town minutes spoke of a "town marshal." George E. Waters observed that from 1910 to 1920, when Gaithersburg's population was less than 1,000, traffic court was presided over by Judge Garrett, justice of the peace and the village cobbler.

Wanting a more professional system, Mayor Merton F. Duvall signed a resolution on April 1, 1963 creating the Gaithersburg police department. It specified a traffic unit to be created within the department, though the new unit was not formed until approximately 1983. Chief David Marstiller was the first chief of police and initially the only police officer.

The department grew from an authorized strength of three sworn officers and one civilian clerk in the early 1970s, when the city's population was 7,000, to its current complement of 35 sworn officers and other administrative staff. In 1997, the police department added a full-time victim advocate, whose duties include assisting victims of domestic violence and presenting crime prevention information to various citizen groups.

Gaithersburg Police Department became the 258th nationally accredited law enforcement agency on July 31, 1993. The department, remaining committed to complying with national standards, was re-accredited in July of 1998 and July of 2001.

PARKS, RECREATION, AND CULTURE

Recreational opportunities in the City of Gaithersburg have expanded greatly over the years. The parks and recreation system began in 1970 when the city had three parks with a total of 9 acres. Today, the city has 23 parks and 9 recreation facilities that cover 551 acres. Also in Gaithersburg is Seneca Creek State Park, which provides 29 additional acres of park land for the use of Gaithersburg citizens. On the city-owned ground, there are athletic fields, aquatic centers, meeting and class facilities, gymnasiums, fitness facilities, miniature golf, an outdoor performance pavilion, trails, and natural areas. A full range of classes, sports programs, youth activities, cultural arts activities, and special events are also part of the city's parks and recreation department.

In 1999, the city completed work on an ambitious parks, recreation, and open space master plan that calls for the acquisition of additional active park land and the development of new recreation opportunities. In spring 2000, the department was renamed Parks, Recreation, and Culture to include the numerous arts and cultural programs provided by the city.

PLANNING AND CODE ADMINISTRATION

The planning and code administration oversees growth and orderly development within the city and enforces all ordinances and codes that govern residential and commercial construction within the corporate limits. Five teams carry out the functions of the department. The urban design team advises city officials on zoning and development as guided by the master plan, city code, and sound planning principles. Permits and inspections are administered by this department in consideration of environmental and building safety. Neighborhood services include rental housing, landlord-tenant relations, property maintenance, and public nuisances. City residents are provided animal control

This photograph of the Schwartz peony garden was taken in 1913.

services including licensing, education, and rabies clinics. An administrative team coordinates publications and other administrative work of the planning and code department. Planning and code department staff serve as liaisons to the city's planning commission, which advises the mayor and council on matters of zoning, development and redevelopment.

FINANCE AND ADMINISTRATION

The finance and administration department's responsibilities include the receipt and disbursement of city funds; financial reporting; investment of idle funds; control of fixed assets; collection of taxes and assessments for special projects; assisting all departments in securing supplies, materials, equipment, and services; and providing employee services such as maintenance of personnel, group hospitalization, life insurance, and retirement records. Its duties also include assisting the city manager in preparation of the annual budget and supervision of the city insurance program.

INFORMATION TECHNOLOGY

The information technology department provides guidance and support for all of the city's computer equipment, telephone systems, geographic information systems, and related information systems, which benefit all city departments. This department continues to ride the wave of technology to provide services to Gaithersburg citizens and others and to facilitate more interaction between citizens, the mayor and council, all city departments, and employees using e-government solutions that provide customer service 24 hours a day, seven days a week. Examples of these include a touch-tone telephone voice response system used to register for programs and building inspections; another telephone system, Answer Line, gives information 24 hours a day, seven days a week; and with city geographic information, staff can enter an address and get zoning, property tax, recycling day, and other pertinent information for each city property.

PUBLIC WORKS, PARK MAINTENANCE, AND ENGINEERING

This department provides a variety of services such as snow removal; street sweeping; repair and maintenance of streets, sidewalks, and storm drains; beautification and maintenance of the city's streets, public buildings, and parks; recycling; city vehicle maintenance; and storm water management.

It also is in charge of maintaining all city facilities including custodial services, utilities, repairs, supervision of construction, and service contracts for all major equipment. Engineering functions include reviews of storm water management, sediment control, storm drainage, paving, and site plans for new developments.

11. Olde Towne and Revitalization

The area called "Olde Towne" was developed as a commercial and residential neighborhood after the B&O Railroad arrived in 1873, and it encompasses stores and residences in the Diamond, Summit Park, Russell, Brookes, and Walker Avenues area. Most of the shops are family owned and operated rather than chain stores, which adds to the strong hometown atmosphere.

The intersection of Diamond and Summit Avenues served as Gaithersburg's commercial center from 1880 to 1980, when Lakeforest Regional Mall was opened and neighborhood shopping centers proliferated. The railroad brought prosperity to Olde Towne and some buildings from that flourishing era remain today. Unfortunately, fires in the early 1900s destroyed many architecturally significant buildings and led to major remodeling of others.

The 1894 map delineating the corporate limits of Gaithersburg shows that major landowners within Olde Towne included John B. Diamond, W.R. Hutton, John A. Belt, J.H. Nicholls, Rosa Miller, and the Gaithersburg Milling and Manufacturing Company. Russell Avenue, in the block between Diamond and Brookes, was completely occupied by 1894. Park Avenue was regarded as a compound of the McBain and Carlisle families. William Carlisle built 16 Park Avenue around 1890.

William McBain was mayor of Gaithersburg for 22 years, longer by far than any other mayor. During his entire term in office he lived in a house at 4 Park Avenue. McBain's daughter married Roger Carlisle and they built their own home on Park. Mayor McBain speculated in a small way by building at 11 and 13 Park Avenue in the latter part of the 1930s. These duplex houses have now been renovated for office use.

Fortunately, the four major turn-of-the-century buildings at the intersection of Diamond and Summit Avenues have survived. However, if not for the 1891 date on the First National Bank building and the familiar gable on the 1894 Etchison's (Diamond) Drug Store, these two historic buildings might be difficult to recognize. The bank has lost its original steepled roofline and the drug store now incorporates the adjacent 1874 Diamond Hall and Nicholls's Harness Shop behind an extended front facade. On the southern corners, the 1903 J.A. Belt Building and the 1884 B&O Railroad Station and Freight House have been restored and retain their original appearance. Both are on the National Register of Historic Places.

Other notable historic buildings that have been preserved and adapted for use as offices include the Gartner Funeral Home and the residences at 316 and 320 East Diamond

This turn-of-the-century photograph shows Diamond Avenue in a view looking west toward the Belt Building.

Avenue, and the Exchange Building at 124 East Diamond Avenue, which has been designated a local historic site.

By 2001, most of the former residences in Olde Towne were in small office or commercial use. At times, great efforts were made to preserve older buildings for the future.

In 1985, when plans were approved for Kay Bowling's Diamond Oak apartment project on the west side of Russell Avenue, she moved Dr. Broschart's historic house and office at 8 Russell Avenue across the street to become 7 Russell Avenue. It filled a hole in the streetscape and was renovated for offices.

During the 1970s, when Gaithersburg was entering its era as a "corridor city," the downtown business owners and the city began a serious assessment of the future role of the Diamond and Summit commercial area. The city worked with Montgomery County, and in 1979, the Olde Towne area was designated as a federal Housing and Urban Development Neighborhood Strategy Area eligible for Community Development Block Grant–funded improvements.

The city then contracted the consulting firm of Barton-Aschman to prepare a revitalization plan for the Victorian downtown. Although not implemented in its entirety, the report offered key recommendations that served as the basis for the first efforts at the revitalization of Olde Towne and, most importantly, saved it from demolition. The study recognized the historical and present importance of the East Diamond Avenue commercial area and strongly recommended the use of design guidelines to improve the appearance and environment through public- and private-funded improvements.

As part of the 1985 master plan, the row of turn-of-the-century frame houses on the north side of East Diamond Avenue was rezoned from medium density residential to residential buffer. The previous zoning encouraged the assembling of old residential properties for redevelopment as apartment complexes, while the new zoning permitted office and low-profile uses. Many people believed that parking was the major stumbling block to the revitalization of Olde Towne, and to alleviate this problem, the city spent approximately $400,000 to purchase, improve, and lease properties within the Diamond/Summit commercial area for public parking.

In 1981, the mayor and city council adopted a set of general guidelines and appointed a downtown review committee to oversee the revitalization project. City staff, the downtown review committee, and the chamber of commerce worked with property owners to help them through the project's design and construction phase. Community Development Block Grant funds were used to purchase building facade easements in return for contributing part of the cost of storefront and signage improvements.

The revitalization of buildings started in 1981, and on Sunday, September 26, 1982, Gaithersburg celebrated its first Olde Towne Day, a community festival to celebrate the revitalization and to foster appreciation for Gaithersburg's heritage. Special recognition was given to W. Lawson King, who was the first Olde Towne property owner to revitalize his buildings under the city's new program. Thirty-four Olde Towne storefronts were improved under the easement program. City Hall, the Wells-Robertson House, the Belt Building, and the B&O station are other major improvement projects that have been completed outside of the program.

On February 4, 1991, Governor William Donald Schaefer announced that Olde Towne Gaithersburg was officially designated as one of the state's first Maryland Main Street Communities. He applauded Gaithersburg officials and staff for their hard work and the strong spirit of cooperation demonstrated by merchants, business professionals, and residents in their successful efforts to revitalize and preserve the small-town character of Gaithersburg's Victorian business and residential district.

In 1995, the city began the second phase of the revitalization project with a blueprint for Olde Towne that led to the designation of a central business district with flexible zoning and incentives for investment and commerce in Olde Towne. The new policies resulted in the construction of two award-winning office buildings on South Summit Avenue, a pavilion for the performing arts at City Hall, a much needed parking structure with an elevated walkway across the tracks to the business district, and new apartment development. The new revitalization is aimed at preserving the charm of Olde Towne while attracting new residents, jobs, and shopping to the downtown.

THE BELT BUILDING

The Belt Building at the intersection of Diamond and Summit Avenues carries the name J.A. Belt and the construction date of 1903 on the east elevation parapet. Belt proudly dated and signed this structure when he rebuilt his earlier two-story frame structure, which had been completely destroyed by fire in September 1903. At the time, Belt was considered the leading merchant in Gaithersburg with one of the county's largest mercantile businesses. The Belt Building is both a local historic site and on the National Register of Historic Places.

John A. Belt was first recorded as a Gaithersburg merchant in the *Sentinel* on April 18, 1879, when a robbery was reported at his store "opposite the depot." The precise location of this first store is not known. Belt was not only a successful and prosperous merchant but also Gaithersburg's postmaster from 1885 to 1890 and again from 1893 to 1897. He was elected to serve as a member of the town's board of commissioners from 1890 to 1894.

Belt purchased three residential lots on East Diamond Avenue from William Hutton in 1879, 1884, and 1886. One was for his home and one was for his mother-in-law, Mary Anderson. These lots were not within the town limits, which ended roughly at the corner of Diamond and Summit at that time. Therefore, he was not a town resident and not eligible to vote, hold office, or influence town affairs. A motion was recorded in the town minutes of February 20, 1888 "to appoint a committee to take into consideration the extension of the Corporation limits as prayed for by Mr. John A. Belt and others." Belt's property was included in the 1888 annexation, and he became a legal resident.

Now with a voice in the progress of the town, Belt proceeded to buy property on the southwest side of Diamond and Summit Avenues from J.S. Poole early in 1889. The *Sentinel* reported on September 6, 1889 that "Mr. John A. Belt, a leading merchant of Gaithersburg, has commenced the erection at that place of a large store-house. . . . The building, when completed will be one of the largest in the county."

This store and its public hall, Norman Hall, immediately became the pivotal structure of Gaithersburg's social, cultural, and governmental activities as well as the town's post office. Norman Hall was home to the Waverly Literary Society, and its library and stage were used for theater performances, lectures, recitals, musical presentations, and high school graduations.

After lightning destroyed the Diamond Hall Masonic Lodge in May 1898, the *Sentinel* reported on December 29, 1899, "A large hall building 50 x 100 feet is being erected at Gaithersburg by John A. Belt." This substantiates the Belt family's story that Belt donated $1,500 toward building the new Masonic Hall at 8 Russell Avenue. His generosity to the Masons and his extension of credit to those in need, coupled with his losses from a disastrous fire, probably caused the failure of his Gaithersburg business.

Unfortunately, Belt was in Westminster, Maryland when a fire broke out in his storehouse on September 15, 1903. Store employees were driven out by exploding ammunition without being able to salvage any property, goods, or business records. Belt purchased 9,500 red bricks from the Gaithersburg Milling and Manufacturing Company on October 12 that same year and constructed a new fireproof building during the last three months of 1903. He never recovered financially from the loss of his stock and store, however. In 1904, the *Sentinel* reported, "Mr. J.A. Belt, the oldest established merchant in Gaithersburg, this county, voluntarily executed a deed of trust to Atty. Wm. H. Talbott on Wednesday for the benefit of his creditors."

Marshall Walker managed the business until the building was sold at auction to George Linthicum for $8,100 on March 21, 1914. In 1915, Forest Walker and Clay Plummer purchased the store. Soon after, Marshall Walker, Belt's former manager, acquired Plummer's interest and the store continued as the Walker Store until the early 1950s. The Belt building had many different uses over the years. W. Lawson King started King Motor Co. (later King Pontiac) at the Belt Building in 1929, and it also housed a restaurant, photographer, flower shop, and pizzeria over the years.

When the city launched the Olde Towne revitalization in the 1980s, this building was vacant and without on-site parking. Strategies were formulated to provide incentives for restoration and reuse, one of which resulted in parking waiver legislation for this and other pre-automotive buildings. Of equal importance was the city Historic Preservation Advisory Committee's assistance with the National Register designation to make restoration costs certifiable for the lucrative 25 percent investment tax credit. In 1988, an addition was made to the rear and the restoration was completed. In 1993, the J.A. Belt Building was again renovated and a side dining room with a roof terrace was added to furnish a home to Montgomery County's first microbrewery restaurant.

J.A. Belt built his first store on Diamond and Summit Avenues in 1879. This one, built in 1903, replaced the original when it was lost in a fire.

Thus, Belt's store has come full circle. It is a reminder to this generation that more than a century ago, people with ambition and aspirations built structures to accommodate their dreams and left a tangible legacy of other times for us to enjoy.

GRAIN MILLS AND THE CANNERY

Once the cornerstone of Olde Towne Gaithersburg, the grain mills and the cannery are again playing a dominant role in the the the redevelopment of the city's original mercantile district. Strategically placed along the B&O railway line, the mills ensured a steady supply of crops for processing and were instrumental in transforming a fledgling agricultural town into a commercial agricultural hub. Today, the same buildings that housed Olde Towne's economic essence more than three-quarters of a century ago are set to resume their role of establishing and sustaining a solid business base in Olde Towne's central business district.

The Bowman Brothers Mill, built by the Bowman Brothers in 1919, exemplifies the concept of endurance. The mill, at 401 East Diamond Avenue, was twice destroyed by fire, once in 1943 and again in 1987. Today, the facility hosts office, restaurant, and retail tenants. Purchased in 1993 by a local business owner/developer, the mill proved a worthy

Gaithersburg Milling and Manufacturing is in Olde Towne. (Courtesy of T. Irving Fulks.)

challenge. All the feed bins lining the railway side of the building were still intact, as were the auger, used for grinding feed, and the grain distribution machine. According to the owner, the most rewarding aspect of the redevelopment was "taking something that nobody else wanted and turning it into a successful office/retail complex." The mill, renamed Granary Row, was the winner of the 1997 Merit Award by the Maryland Society of American Institute of Architects.

Thomas & Company Cannery was the first, largest, and longest-operating food cannery in Montgomery County and the only sizable industry in Gaithersburg. It provided a local market for area farmers and jobs and income to the community. Fire damaged the cannery building in 1962 when local agricultural production was waning in favor of suburban development, and the cannery operation was not resumed. The 1917 brick cannery and storehouse building retains its characteristic World War I–era industrial architectural features.

The cannery was built on a large parcel of land on Chestnut Street extending along the B&O tracks at Ward's Station, conveniently located for rail shipping and receiving. The cannery building consisted of the production line, kettles for preparing the vegetables, fillers, cappers, cookers, and a cold water cooling canal from the factory to the finished goods warehouse. The warehouse has been rebuilt and is used by Standard Supply.

The factory originally canned corn and pumpkin, then peas and corn. The pea season lasted for four to six weeks beginning in late May or June, followed by a six-week slack time, then by corn production until October. The product was put into gallon cans for wholesale and institutional sale.

The operation employed about 200 people when canning. It took approximately 130 to 140 people to run the line. Students were paid 25¢ to 50¢ an hour for preparation in the 1940s and 1950s, and those holding more responsible positions received up to $1 per hour in the mid-1950s. Many people worked shifts for several days a week, but during the height of the season when the operation continued until all produce was processed, some people worked from opening at 5:00 or 6:00 a.m. until midnight or later.

The cannery had a ripple effect on the Gaithersburg economy. Laborers, field workers, and pickers were needed to cultivate and harvest peas and sweet corn for the plant. Truckers and administrative and sales representatives were needed to transport and sell the product. Local workers captured the bulk of the jobs until the late 1950s when migrant workers were first employed in field and production work. Alternative cannery crops created a more stable farm economy than one based exclusively on dairying or grain production.

The income from seasonal farm labor and cannery production was in turn pumped back into Gaithersburg's strong farm supply and retail businesses. While Frank Thomas ran the cannery, his brother Clyde took care of Thomas and Co. Hardware to supply local farmers with the products they would need. Gaithersburg Rental now stands where this hardware store was located.

During the World War II era, manpower was scarce because of armed service demands. A German prisoner of war camp was established near Gaithersburg, roughly at the intersection of Goshen and Snouffers School Roads. POWs were utilized to keep the operation running, largely in the fields, but some also worked in the cannery operation in Gaithersburg.

There were some drawbacks to such an industry operating in the small town. The odor from production waste and residue could become pungent enough in the hot and humid summers to overpower most of the town, and drainage was a problem from the start. A filtration plant was installed, but this never completely alleviated the problem. Neighbors appealed to the mayor and council for relief on occasion, but the situation was always resolved without drastic action.

In 1956, the cannery was acquired from the Thomas heirs by Jenkins Bros. Cannery Company of Frederick. Migrant workers were brought from Florida to work at the plant and were housed in frame dormitories within the cannery complex. In 1958, a fire broke out in a dormitory, killing an infant. The City of Gaithersburg notified the cannery that the housing must be removed. Another fire broke out there in June 1962, doing $10,000 in damage. A resident on West Diamond Avenue, several blocks away, recalled that the sound of the exploding cans was "like shots being fired or firecrackers exploding."

The fire investigation revealed that 15 migrant workers had been present, housed in a "chicken-coop-like structure within the confines of Jenkins Bros. Cannery Company." The city again ordered Jenkins Bros. to remove workers and the substandard dormitories or face legal action. The loss of low-cost labor together with the waning of local agriculture was a heavy double blow and the cannery operation was not restarted. The smokestack and some portions of the cannery complex were taken down. The main building remained vacant until recently, when it was renovated and refitted to house stores.

Neighboring mills are also filling retail and service niches. The Bryant Mill, more commonly known as Williams Feed and Supply, was originally a provider of poultry and livestock feed, grain, and fertilizer. The massive hand-hewn beams and a multitude of sorting bins still exist and serve as a testament to its original use. The owner currently leases the space to unique sales and service providers.

The Fulks Store/Feed Mill, constructed as a working feed mill and later leased for the same purpose, was acquired and enlarged by W. Lawson King and operated for many years as Gaithersburg Farmers' Supply. Currently, a truck accessories business and a glass company share the site at 451 and 453 East Diamond Avenue.

THE CHESTNUT AND MEEM HISTORIC DISTRICT

The stories of Meem's addition to Gaithersburg and Crawfordtown illustrate the nineteenth-century speculation and development boom around Gaithersburg that both preceded and followed the 1873 opening of the B&O Railroad. A number of structures built between the 1870s and 1930 remain in this area and many are in nearly original condition. The houses along Chestnut Street and along Meem Avenue west of the tracks were designated as a Gaithersburg historic district in 1997.

The Chestnut/Meem neighborhood is bounded by Avenel Business Park on the northwest, West Diamond Avenue on the west and south, and Frederick Avenue on the east. Historically, the neighborhood was a mixed residential and commercial area along Frederick Avenue and an agricultural area elsewhere. When the railroad arrived in 1873, residences began to be built west of the tracks.

The land along Chestnut Street and West Diamond Avenue is part of two eighteenth-century farms, Zoar and Rawlings Rest. These large plantations had been carved into smaller pieces by 1862, when George and Martha Meem came to Gaithersburg from Georgetown and Martha purchased 200 acres from Mary J. Bibb for $5 per acre. George died October 13, 1865, and shortly thereafter, Martha began to sell off parcels of her land. In 1868, the railroad condemned a 7-acre right-of-way strip through Mrs. Meem's property, which increased its value as commercial and residential land. At this point, Chestnut Street did not exist. However, in 1873, Henry C. Ward and Ignatius Fulks purchased several parcels of land totaling more than 4 acres near the tracks for the firm of Ward and Fulks. One deed included the right to open, maintain, and use a 30-foot-wide road connecting their land to the Barnesville (West Diamond) Road. Ward and Fulks also bought a lot that was developed with a four-square house at 24 West Diamond that still stands on West Diamond Avenue adjacent to the Mathias Service Center.

Chestnut Street was originally built to access Ward's Station at the railroad tracks. However, it also provided a direct route to Ward and Fulks Store at 205 North Frederick Avenue near Chestnut. Soon it became the preferred way to get from Darnestown or Quince Orchard to Gaithersburg without crossing the dangerous Frederick Avenue intersection with the railroad tracks. Chestnut Street became a county road in 1883.

Martha Meem clearly intended her property to be developed as a prestigious neighborhood with grand houses. In 1879, she built the imposing and stylish, French

The Meem family sits in front of Martha Meem's house in this early photograph.

Jacob Wolfson, grandfather of Mayor Sidney A. Katz, is shown in his Diamond Avenue department store in this 1932 photograph.

Second Empire–inspired house at 104 Chestnut Street. Farmer John Wesley Briggs purchased the property at 102 Chestnut from Harry Meem in 1902 and built the neighboring Victorian house for his retirement home. Other prominent houses include the front-gabled house at 105 Chestnut, built by Charles Beall Jr. after 1910, and the Craftsman bungalow at 115 Chestnut, built in 1912 by Abell Norris.

Meem Avenue landmarks include the Robertson House at 115 Meem that was built in 1911 and the bungalow built by Aubrey and Susie Mills at 106 Meem. The house at 108 Meem was built around 1920, and the Kole Cottage at 113 Meem was built in the late 1920s. Many have retained the ancient trees, shrubs, and old outbuildings that give the area a well-settled atmosphere.

Crawfordtown was built on another portion of the original 200-acre Meem property. It was acquired by Charles C. Crawford through a tax sale in 1909, but it is not clear whether Crawford built the five vernacular two-story frame houses on the parcel or if they were already there at the time of the purchase. The only remnants of Crawfordtown were located at 300 and 304 West Diamond Avenue, but these structures were removed in 2000 when the state highway administration widened West Diamond Avenue.

More than a century after Martha Meem purchased her 200-acre investment, the City of Gaithersburg designated the Chestnut Street and Meem Avenue houses a historic district to protect this highly visible evidence of the city's development history. The succession of period building styles, tall trees, and streets of the original Meem subdivision, and especially the grand old house that Martha built, provide a welcoming entrance to Gaithersburg's Olde Towne.

BROWN'S STATION

Before 1845, Thomas and Jane Patterson owned the land where Brown's Station was built. In 1846, it was purchased by Mary Bibb, whose husband, George M. Bibb, was a U.S. senator from Kentucky who was appointed secretary of the U.S. Treasury in 1844. After his term of office, Bibb practiced law in the District of Columbia and was an assistant in the office of the U.S. attorney general.

The Bibbs lived in Georgetown, but Mrs. Bibb bought 230 acres of land from the Pattersons in 1846 for a summer home, which the couple named Pomona (meaning "fruitful"). The property was on the corner of Clopper Road and (later) Brown Station Road. Mrs. Bibb continued to purchase land and eventually owned most of the land between Route 355 and West Diamond Avenue from the railroad in Gaithersburg to Quince Orchard Road.

Mrs. Bibb's daughter Caroline Matilda Bibb (born *c.* 1839) married Thomas J. Brown on October 10, 1866, and Thomas and Caroline inherited Pomona from Mary Bibb in 1875. By that time, the Metropolitan Branch of the B&O Railroad had cut through their land and 200 acres had been sold in 1864 to another Georgetown family, George and Martha Meem, who lived at Mt. Washington on the south side of the tracks.

When the railroad came to Gaithersburg in 1873 almost everyone wanted to live close to the train to get to work, ship farm products, or go shopping and visiting. In 1894, Thomas and Caroline Brown established a railroad station on their property and hoped to start a residential community. This "station" was not a fancy brick building, but a small passenger shelter. It was used for many years, but large housing developments were not built near Brown Station until the 1970s.

To get people to the station, Brown's Station Road was cut through from Route 355 to the intersection of Clopper and Quince Orchard Roads. Although it was intended to serve the railroad station, it was a handy shortcut from Clopper Road to Frederick Avenue and became a well-used route. The road's name was changed to Montgomery Village Avenue in the 1970s.

Brown Station Elementary School was the first new elementary school in expanded Gaithersburg. There were few schools outside Gaithersburg before Brown Station Elementary was built. Most of the small schools were one- or two-room primary schools that educated only to the eighth grade. Brown Station Elementary was planned for use as a summer recreation center as well as a school. It was also one of the first modifiable "open space" plans with the media center in the middle of four radiating wings. Eighteen classrooms, two kindergartens, an all-purpose room, and other facilities were finished in 1969. The school used innovative methods to go with its design—it used team teaching and was largely non-graded. Eight more classrooms and a gym were added in 1974.

THE BROOKES, RUSSELL, AND WALKER HISTORIC DISTRICT

During the city's centennial year in 1978, Gaithersburg was undergoing rapid urbanization, and the widening of Frederick Avenue was removing most of the small-town streetscape and many older structures. A number of citizens banded together to propose a historic district encompassing the remaining pocket of residential and commercial portions of old Gaithersburg. The residents of the proposed district encouraged the mayor and council to enact historic legislation, and after several drafts and boundary revisions, the long-awaited Preservation of Historic Resources Ordinance was finally adopted in 1981.

The first draft of the proposed district ran from Maryland to Brookes Avenues and included Russell Avenue and Park to Diamond Avenues, generally following an area labeled "Old Gaithersburg" in the Maryland–National Capital Park and Planning Commission's historic sites inventory. After several public meetings held by the Historic Preservation Advisory Committee, the boundaries were redrawn to exclude commercial properties and Olde Towne, and the new area was designated as the city's first historic district. The geographical area encompasses 54 buildings on Walker and Brookes Avenues linked by the west side of Russell Avenue.

Forty-nine Victorian and early-twentieth-century buildings line the tree-canopied avenues. The predominant character of the district is set by rows of two-and-one-half story vernacular houses with front porches and emphasized front gables. Stylistic features found throughout the district include tin roofs, bay windows, wood siding with fish scale trim, porches with gingerbread brackets, colonial revival columns, and widow's walks.

Brookes Avenue has six houses constructed before 1894, although one, Carson Ward's late-1890s home at 6 Brookes Avenue, was demolished for Carson Ward Store parking in 1985. The Moore-Bell House at 24 Brookes, built in 1895, is still an outstanding landmark possessing the richest Queen Anne–style architectural detail in the district. It was designed by Victorian architect George Franklin Barber and was built for Louis and Virginia Bell by Mrs. Bell's uncle Tom Moore from Virginia.

The original Epworth Methodist Episcopal Church at 14 Brookes Avenue was built in 1891 from an approved plan for a "handsome and commodious edifice." In 1990, the church that then owned the building applied for a historic area work permit and received approval to construct a large rear addition for an assembly room.

The block of Russell between Brookes and Walker is a cluster of late-nineteenth-century homes on large lots that exhibit the charm that draws new residents to the area. The large Victorian home at 104 Russell was built in 1892 by R.W. Thompson. It was bequeathed by Dr. A. Contee Thompson in 1968 to Ascension Church and was used as a home for teenagers needing foster care. Today, the house has been restored and returned to its original use as a private residence. After a long process, heated discussion, and several lawsuits, its two vacant side-yard lots at the corner were developed with new houses that are eminently compatible and comfortable with the surrounding district's houses.

Walker Avenue is the most cohesive street in the historic district. Most of its houses were built between 1904 and 1930. Only one was built later, in 1950. The lots on this street are unusually deep in order to carry the lot lines to the edge of the original field and also to provide space for chickens and gardens. The street is named for John Wesley Walker, whose farm lane became Walker Avenue when he subdivided the front part of his farm in 1904. Walker Avenue received electric streetlights on June 11, 1913 and was the first street in town to have this amenity for its full length.

Many important government leaders lived on Walker Avenue. John Wesley Walker was mayor of Gaithersburg from 1906 to 1908 and again from 1918 to 1924. Four other mayors lived on Walker Avenue. John Wesley Walker's son-in-law Walter Magruder built 101 Walker Avenue. Magruder was mayor from 1924 to 1926 following his father-in-law's term. Walker Avenue resident Harry C. Perry took over the mayor's job from 1948 to 1954. Mayor Perry and his large family lived at no. 18. Milton Walker, mayor from 1974 to 1976, spent his boyhood at 11 Walker Avenue, and mayor W. Edward Bohrer Jr. lived at 11 Walker early in his married life.

Other notable residents of the street included the two men most responsible for the Asbury Home. The Reverend J.J. Ringer, first superintendent of the Asbury Home, lived at no. 16, and Reverend Herman Wilson, who expanded the Asbury complex, lived at the former Magruder house at 101 Walker Avenue. The Magruder-Wilson house was moved in 1986 to 100 Prospect Avenue. Charles M. Orme, chief of police of Montgomery County, lived at 20 Walker Avenue. Crittenden Walker, a member of the house of

This turn-of-the-century photograph shows Summit Avenue in a view looking west toward the train station.

137

delegates, lived at no. 25, and no. 30 was owned by Professor Thomas W. Troxell, superintendent of Gaithersburg's schools for many years.

In 1988, Mayor Bohrer received a letter from the National Park Service certifying that the Brookes, Russell, and Walker Historic District substantially met all the requirements for the listing of districts in the National Register of Historic Places.

ASBURY VILLAGE

Although outside the boundary line of the district, the lawns and gardens of the original Asbury Methodist Home contribute to the beauty and history of the area. The present Asbury Village is a complex of brick buildings located on a 130-acre tract between Olde Towne and Lakeforest Mall. In 2001, the non-profit organization celebrated 75 years as an innovator in continuing care for people 65 years and older, with special emphasis on improving the quality of life for the residents.

In 1921, the Baltimore Conference of the Methodist Episcopal Church South named five trustees to look into plans for a home for the aged of the conference. The original trustees included a young man, Herman Wilson, who was president of the Conference Epworth League. The trustees were offered the former Gaither/John Wesley Walker farm on the edge of Gaithersburg owned, at that time, by Walker's son-in-law Walter Magruder. When this choice was presented to the Baltimore Conference, "The vote was unanimously in favor of the beautiful farm of Walter M. Magruder, Gaithersburg, MD.,

The Asbury Home for the Aged and Orphans was built in 1928 on the Magruder farm.

in the heart of Montgomery County. It contains 106 acres of land beautiful for situation," according to the conference minutes from 1923.

The farm known as Rolling Acres, with access from Walker Avenue, was purchased for $25,000. Herman Wilson challenged the young people of the church's Epworth League to raise the money, and they succeeded. Architect Rossell Edward Mitchell designed the main building to provide accommodations for 50 persons who could not entirely care for themselves. Independent residents were to live in small cottages scattered around the grounds. The first building was constructed at a cost of $100,000 and had quarters for 70 residents, a dining room, and a reception room. Cottages were built on Russell Avenue for the superintendent and secretary, but the idea of cottages for residents was abandoned.

On April 15, 1926, the Home for the Aged and Orphans of the Baltimore Conference of the Methodist Episcopal Church South, Inc., opened its doors with the Reverend J.J. Ringer as superintendent. On this date, the first five elderly guests came to live at the home. According to Asbury's record, the facility never housed orphans or children.

In 1928, Reverend Wilson became superintendent. With the support of his devoted wife, Lillian, he served more than 40 years in Asbury's ministry to the elderly. Also in 1928, the Baltimore Conference Epworth League raised sufficient money to construct a new wing, to be known as Epworth Hall. Epworth provided 11 additional bedrooms and many home-like amenities including a library, living room, sun porch, social hall, and chapel.

In keeping with the 1938 reunion of the North and South factions of the Methodist Church, Asbury's name was changed in 1940 to the Asbury Methodist Home, Inc. Another merger was soon to follow. In 1945, the Baltimore Conference decided to merge two Westminster homes, which needed substantial repairs, with the Gaithersburg home. The new corporation was called the Asbury Methodist Home for the Aged, Inc.

A new wing, Cassell Hall, was added to accommodate the residents transferred from Westminster. Miss Carrie M. Young donated funds in 1953 for the building and upkeep of the Young Memorial wing, which doubled the home's capacity, but more space was still needed. In June 1955, two more wings were dedicated: Westminster Hall, a residential hall named after the former home; and the Guild Hall, a dining room wing made possible by a donation from the Asbury Home Guild. During the 1960s, the Asbury Home Guild again contributed $150,000 to remodel the basement of the main building into "Williamsburg Lane" with a U.S. Post Office branch station, antique displays, a beauty shop, an ice cream parlor, a gift shop, a hat shop, and the approximately 1,200-piece Luta S. Ferrell doll collection, named for its donor who moved to Asbury in 1952. The Williamsburg Lane project was completed in 1962 and has delighted many visitors since then. It has since moved into the new Cultural Arts and Wellness Center.

Dr. Herman Wilson took the position of administrator emeritus and chaplain in 1963, when his son Ronald H. Wilson became administrator of Asbury. Five years later Dr. Wilson was inducted into the Methodist Hall of Fame in philanthropy. In 1968, the name of the facility was changed again, this time to Asbury Methodist Home, Inc. The next year the board of trustees authorized a planning and development committee to proceed with a total site plan for Asbury Methodist Village. Their plan provided for three 125-unit apartment buildings with their own dining and recreation buildings, a chapel, 20 townhouses, and the 240-bed Herman Wilson Health Care Center. All were to be developed in campus fashion with the lake as the focal point.

The campus began to take form in 1972 but was developed to a higher capacity than expected in the plan. The Norman L. Trott Apartments opened with 125 studio and two-bedroom apartments plus living and dining rooms. In 1977, the 134-unit Edwards-Fisher Apartment Building was opened. The two buildings were connected by the Apartment Center, a central reception and dining area where residents meet for one main meal a day and many other activities.

The 120-bed Herman M. Wilson Health Care Center opened in 1975. It includes physical, recreational, and occupational therapy centers; x-ray, laboratory, dental, podiatry, and dermatology services; kitchen and pharmacological departments; offices and meeting rooms; as well as the patients' rooms. The center also contains a chapel with a stained-glass window designed by Henry Lee Willet. The center was soon filled with patients and an additional 159 beds were added in 1980.

The Wilson Health Care Center housed the administrative offices until June 1986, when Wilson Hall in the original main building was renovated for office use. This project proposed demolition of the Walter Magruder/Herman Wilson House at 101 Walker Avenue in order to widen the entrance to the administrative offices. The city's Historic District Commission encouraged Asbury to offer the historic house for sale to a buyer who would move the structure. The house was purchased and moved to 100 Prospect Avenue that year. The health care building office space was renovated for six short-term patient beds.

In 1981, Asbury Village received two honors: the Agency of the Year award from the National Association of Health and Welfare Ministries, and the Hobart Jackson Award for Affirmative Action and Quality of Care for the Elderly from the American Association of Homes for the Aging. That was also the year in which Ronald Wilson resigned after having served 18 years as administrator; Norman E. Amtower was appointed executive director. Dr. Herman M. Wilson died the next year in 1982.

Asbury opened the 133-unit Mund Apartment Building in 1979, the new Asbury Home with 196 suites in 1984, and in 1993, an apartment building at 415 Russell Avenue was named the Clark Gates and Elizabeth Hoge Diamond Apartment in honor of residents Mr. and Mrs. Clark G. Diamond. In 1992, Asbury broke ground for 73 independent living cottages with garages, called the Villas, on 15 acres across from the Wilson Health Care Center. In 1994, Asbury, with 1,300 residents, saw continuing progress with the completion of its loop road, the planning of Villas Phase II, the renovation of Westminster and Young Halls, and the completion of a study to accommodate new approaches to assisted living.

12. The Twenty-First Century

Gaithersburg's population grew almost 10 times from 1900 to 2000. Officially, the 2000 population was 52,616. The change in the socio-economic structure of the area brought an influx of people to Gaithersburg over the years. First, the federal government and its supporting companies made Gaithersburg a Washington, D.C. suburban town. Then, as technology grew, so did the city's business profile.

Now, Gaithersburg is strategically located in the heart of the Interstate 270 technology corridor and the Washington/Baltimore region. It is a headquarters for internationally known biotechnology and computer services companies serving industry and the federal government. Gaithersburg's Economic Development Office refers to the city as a "biotechnology hub" and "Maryland's technology address." Dedicated to providing the best quality of life, the city offers businesses a stable, attractive community.

Gaithersburg has become a global city, as well, and 2000 census figures indicate a population that is 19.8 percent Hispanic, 14.6 percent African American, and 13.8 percent Asian, with the remainder made up of other races including whites. A study published by the Brookings Institute in 2001 identified Gaithersburg's 20878 zip code as one of the top-ten destinations for immigrants in the Washington metropolitan area. The variety of immigrants to the area include people from El Salvador, Vietnam, India, China, the Philippines, South Korea, Iran, Pakistan, and Peru, along with 116 other countries.

The Maryland State Highway Administration began planning the widening of Frederick Avenue as part of the improvement of Route 355 in 1977. The road was widened from two lanes with parallel parking on the side to a six-lane divided highway with 10-foot public sidewalks on each side. Father Cuddy Bridge was lengthened and rebuilt to six lanes. All of the street trees and most front lawns in this area were removed. Most of the nineteenth-century structures were demolished.

For the first time, utility poles, wires, and signs became the major visual features of Gaithersburg's main street. Since the completion of the widening project in the mid-1980s, the city has implemented a street tree and median planting program and has adopted a sign ordinance. It is now developing a plan for Frederick Avenue that will reestablish it as Gaithersburg's main street and will showcase 200 years of commerce and community development for the twenty-first century.

The city has grown to occupy 10 square miles and many retail centers have been built to serve the community. The indoor shopping center, Lakeforest, anchored by four large department stores with 160 other stores has a 500-seat eatery with many cafes. Gaithersburg Square sits in the midst of much activity on Route 355; shops in Olde Towne offer one-of-a-kind gifts, handmade crafts, and antiques and collectibles. Gaitherstowne Plaza on Route 355 has many one-stop shopping conveniences; the Rio and Washingtonian Center has become a place for the community to shop, eat, and gather in its 460,000 square feet of retail and restaurants; and Market Square and Kentlands Square combine the modern with the best parts of eighteenth and nineteenth century to offer shopping and dining in the western part of the city. Other centers have a vast selection of retail, restaurant, and commercial business.

City officials helped the growing area meet the needs of its citizens by providing leisure-time activities through the building of an activity center, City Hall concert pavilion, additional active and passive parks, and the expansion of the senior center and youth center in the late 1990s. These and other planned facilities will serve the city well into the twenty-first century.

Gaithersburg has grown to be one of the largest cities in Maryland. Overseeing growth and development, the city government carefully guides land use decisions. In 2002, the city began updating its master plan. The master plan process will address land use and other elements such as the Smart Growth Policy, Housing Policy, Transportation,

This aerial view of Olde Towne was taken in 1994.

Bikeways and Pedestrian Plans, and Community Facilities and Sensitive Areas. The process will be completed in 2003.

The city supports a healthy, productive environment with clean air and clean water. The role of Gaithersburg's environmental program is to understand environmental concerns, develop strategies, and make decisions consistent with the city's mission and strategic plan that protect and enhance our environmental resources. New environmental standards were adopted in 2001.

Gaithersburg is an edge city of Washington, D.C. The town's rolling fields of wheat are now roads, housing developments, and commercial enterprises, but at the same time a number of historic communities and traditions have been preserved. As the city thrives in this new millennium and continues to grow, it will retain many of the qualities of a small town with a rich diverse heritage.

A city of the twenty-first century, Gaithersburg is very strong, and city officials have pledged to keep it a special place to live, work, learn, and play.

APPENDIX OF ELECTED OFFICIALS

MAYORS OF GAITHERSBURG

George W. Meem, 1898–1904
Carson Ward, 1904–1906
John W. Walker, 1906–1908
E.D. Kingsley, 1908–1912
Richard H. Miles, 1912–1918
   (died *c.* August 1918)
John W. Walker, 1918–1924
   (elected by council)
Walter M. Magruder, 1924–1926
William C. McBain, 1926–1948
Harry C. Perry Sr., 1948–1954
Merton F. Duvall, 1954–1966
   (died conducting council meeting)
John W. Griffith, 1966–1970
   (elected by council)
Harold C. Morris, 1970–1974
Susan E. Nicholson, 1974
Milton M. Walker, 1974–1976
B. Daniel Walder, 1976–1978
Bruce A. Goldensohn, 1978–1986
W. Edward Bohrer, 1986–1998
   (died August 27, 1998)
Sidney A. Katz, 1998 to present
   (elected by council)

BOARDS OF COMMISSIONERS

June 15, 1878
Henry C. Ward, president
William A. Gloyd
James B. Gaither
R.A. Buriss
C.W. Crawford

May 1879 (for year ending April 30, 1880)
Dr. Elisha C. Etchison, president
Samuel S. Gloyd
R.A. Buriss
James B. Gaither
Henry C. Ward

May 1880
Henry C. Ward, president
S. Benton
R.A. Benton
Dr. Elisha C. Etchison
James B. Gaither

May 1881
Samuel S. Gloyd, president
I.T. Fulks
R.G. Dorsey
Giles Easton
C.F. Duvall

May 1882
I.T. Fulks, president
E.G. Duley, elected road supervisor
William G. English
Giles Easton
Samuel S. Gloyd

May 1883
I.T. Fulks, president
Giles Easton
Samuel S. Gloyd
William T. Burriss
C.F. Duvall

May 1884
C.F. Linthicum, president
Samuel S. Gloyd
George W. Meem
Giles Easton
C.F. Duvall

May 1885
George W. Meem, president
E.M. Holand
J.H. Nicholls
Samuel S. Gloyd
J.L. Gloyd

May 1886
E.H. Etchison, president
George W. Meem
Giles Easton
Samuel S. Gloyd
Thomas Groomes

May 1887
Giles Easton, president
S.G. English
Samuel S. Gloyd
John W. Case
George W. Meem

Mayor Merton Duvall, right, made the first direct-dial telephone call to the mayor of Washington Grove in 1959; Robert Davidson watches the historic event.

Mayor W. Edward Bohrer Jr. sits on the backhoe in this 1986 photograph of councilmembers and former mayors breaking ground for the new addition to City Hall.

May 1888 (first election for 2-year terms)
C.F. Hogan, president
S.G. English
John W. Walker
John T. Selby
George W. Meem

May 1890
Dr. Elisha C. Etchison, president
John A. Belt
O.C. Meem
Giles W. Easton
Samuel S. Gloyd

May 1892
Dr. Elisha C. Etchison, president
John A. Belt
O.C. Meem
Samuel S. Gloyd
John W. Walker

May 1894
C.F. Duvall, president
Lee M. Lipscomb
P.M. Smith
Maurice Phebus
John W. Walker

May 1896
H.W. Gladhill, president
J.B. Adams
R.D. Trundle
J.T. Gloyd
R.L. Buxton

GAITHERSBURG COUNCIL MEMBERS

June 1898
Thomas I. Fulks
James T. English
David G. Carlisle
Richard H. Miles

March 10, 1899
English resigned.
Ward elected to serve unexpired term.

May 1900
Thomas I. Fulks
David G. Carlisle
Carson Ward
Richard H. Miles

June 1902
Thomas I. Fulks
David G. Carlisle
Carson Ward
Joseph T. Gloyd
Richard H. Miles

June 1904
James T. Mills
Thomas I. Fulks
Joseph C. Phoebus
Joseph T. Gloyd

June 1906
Joseph C. Phoebus
Thomas I. Fulks
Richard W. Murphy
James A. Mills

June 1908
George A. Gloyd
D.G. Carlisle
David F. Virts
Charles A. Spates

June 1910
George A. Gloyd
David F. Virts
D.G. Carlisle
Charles A. Spates

Gaithersburg celebrated Flag Day in Olde Towne Park in 1991.

June 1912
Carson Ward
John W. Walker
Albert F. Meem
Joseph C. Phoebus

June 1914
Carson Ward
John W. Walker
Joseph C. Phoebus
Albert F. Meem

June 1916
(first election for 4-year staggered terms)
Carson Ward (4 years)
Frank B. Severance (4 years)
John W. Walker (2 years)
Albert F. Meem (2 years)

May 1918
Albert F. Meem (4 years)
John W. Walker (4 years)
Carson Ward (2 years)
Frank B. Severance (2 years)

August 5, 1918
Walker appointed to serve Davis's
    unexpired mayoral term.
Kanode elected to fill Walker's seat.

May 1920
Carson Ward (4 years)
Frank B. Severance (4 years)
Robert E. Kanode (2 years)
Albert F. Meem (2 years)

May 1922
Albert F. Meem (4 years)
Edgar Fulks (4 years)
Carson Ward (2 years)
Frank B. Severance (2 years)

May 1924
Norman B. Jacobs (4 years)
Frank B. Severance (4 years)
Edgar Fulks (2 years)
Albert F. Meem (2 years)

May 1926
Otho C. Trundle (4 years)
Ira Darby (4 years)
Norman B. Jacobs (2 years)
Frank B. Severance (2 years)

May 1928
George W. Marshall (4 years)
C. Leslie Ward (4 years)
Otho C. Trundle (2 years)
Ira Darby (2 years)

May 1930
Ira Darby (4 years)
Otho C. Trundle (4 years)
George W. Marshall (2 years)
C. Leslie Ward (2 years)

May 1932
C. Leslie Ward (4 years)
George W. Marshall (4 years)
Otho C. Trundle (2 years)
Ira Darby (2 years)

May 1934
Otho C. Trundle (4 years)
Ira Darby (4 years)
George W. Marshall (2 years)
C. Leslie Ward (2 years)

December 11, 1934
Darby resigned.
Talbott elected by council to serve
    unexpired term.

This photograph shows Mayor Walter M. Magruder, who served from 1924 to 1926.

This 1930 photograph shows the Schwartz house before it became City Hall.

149

Hattie and Walter, two children of city workers, are playing at Summit Hall in this photograph. (Courtesy of Betty Jeanne Jacobs.)

May 1936
William S. Cooley (4 years)
Hobart H. Ramsdell (4 years)
George W. Marshall (2 years)
Otho C. Trundle (2 years)

May 1938
George W. Marshall (4 years)
Otho C. Trundle (4 years)
Hobart H. Ramsdell (2 years)
William S. Cooley (2 years)

May 1940
Hobart H. Ramsdell (4 years)
Harold W. Ward (4 years)
George W. Marshall (2 years)
Otho C. Trundle (2 years)

May 1942
William A. Waters (4 years)
Otho C. Trundle (4 years)
Hobart H. Ramsdell (2 years)
Harold W. Ward (2 years)

1943
Waters resigned January 4, and Micuda
    served unexpired term.
Ward resigned February 1, and Abel served
    unexpired term.

May 1944
John Micuda (4 years)
Harry C. Perr, Sr. (4 years)
Charles P. Fox (2 years)
Otho C. Trundle (2 years)

May 1946
Charles P. Fox (4 years)
George W. Marshall (4 years)
Samuel B. Briggs (2 years)
Harry C. Perry Sr. (2 years)

May 1948
Samuel B. Briggs (4 years)
Hobart H. Ramsdell (4 years)
George W. Marshall (2 years)
Charles P. Fox (2 years)

December 6, 1948
Ramsdell resigned, and Ward appointed to
   fill unexpired term.

May 1950
Charles P. Fox (4 years)
George W. Marshall (4 years)
G. Sprigg Ward (2 years)
Samuel B. Briggs (2 years)

May 1952
G. Sprigg Ward (4 years)
Samuel B. Briggs (4 years)
George W. Marshall (2 years)
Charles Fox (2 years)

May 1954
John W. Griffith (4 years)
E. Russell Gloyd (4 years)
Samuel B. Briggs (2 years)
G. Sprigg Ward (2 years)

May 1956
Milton M. Walker (4 years)
Rodney M. Thompson (4 years)
E. Russell Gloyd (2 years)
John W. Griffith (2 years)

This 1960 photograph shows vintage fire-fighting equipment.

May 1958
(fifth seat added, all 4-year terms)
E. Russell Gloyd
John S. Thomas
Rodney M. Thompson
John W. Griffith
Milton M. Walker

September 28, 1959
Thompson resigned, and Frey appointed
 to serve unexpired term.

November 2, 1959
Gloyd resigned, and Byrnes appointed to
 serve unexpired term.

October 2, 1961
Thomas resigned, and Hurley appointed
 to serve unexpired term.

May 1962
Quentin V. Frey
John W. Griffith
William N. Hurley Jr.
Harold C. Morris
Milton M. Walker

January 6, 1964
Hurley resigned, and McPherson
 appointed to serve term.

March 7, 1966
Griffith appointed to serve Duvall's
 unexpired mayoral term.
Fulks appointed March 14 to serve
 Griffith's unexpired term.

May 1966
T. Irving Fulks
William M. Fullerton
James W. Hane
Harold C. Morris
Milton M. Walker

June 26, 1967
Morris appointed to serve Griffith's
 unexpired mayoral term.
Shay appointed July 17 to serve Morris's
 unexpired term.

May 1970 (staggered elections)
T. Irving Fulks (2 years)
William M. Fullerton (2 years)
Carroll R. Kearns (4 years)
James R. Shay (2 years)
Milton M. Walker (4 years)

May 1972
T. Irving Fulks (4 years)
William M. Fullerton (4 years)
James R. Shay (4 years)
Milton M. Walker (2 years)
Carroll R. Kearns(2 years)

May 1974
Milton M. Walker (4 years)
Carroll R. Kearns (4 years)
T. Irving Fulks (2 years)
William M. Fullerton (2 years)
James R. Shay (2 years)

October 1974
Walker appointed to serve Nicholson's
 mayoral term.
Spaulding served Walker's unexpired term.

May 1976
W. Edward Bohrer Jr. (4 years)
Bruce A. Goldensohn (4 years)
Edward W. Steudal (4 years)
Arthur E. Spaulding (2 years)
Carroll R. Kearns (2 years)

This Junior Drum and Bugle Corps of the American Legion was photographed in 1939.

May 1978
Sidney A. Katz (4 years)
Gertrude Kildee (4 years)
W. Edward Bohrer Jr. (2 years)
Edward M. Steudal (2 years)
Mary B. Ward (2 years, served
    Goldensohn's term)

May 1980
W. Edward Bohrer Jr. (4 years)
Mary B. Ward (4 years)
Julius J. Persensky (4 years)
Sidney A. Katz (2 years)
Gertrude M. Kildee (2 years)

May 1982
Sidney A. Katz (4 years)
Gertrude M. Kildee (4 years)
W. Edward Bohrer Jr. (2 years)
Mary B. Ward (2 years)
Julius J. Persensky (2 years)

May 1984
W. Edward Bohrer Jr. (4 years)
Mary B. Ward (4 years)
Julius J. Persensky (4 years)
Sidney A. Katz (2 years)
Gertrude M. Kildee (2 years)

May 1986
Sidney A. Katz (4 years)
Gertrude M. Kildee (4 y
Mary B. Ward (2 years)
Julius J. Persensky (2 years)
Stanley J. Alster (2 years)

May 19, 1986
Alster appointed to serve Bohrer's
    unexpired term.

May 1988
Julius J. Persensky (4 years)
Stanley J. Alster (4 years)
Mary B. Ward (4 years)
Sidney A. Katz (2 years)
Gertrude M. Kildee (2 years)

May 1989
Sidney A. Katz (4 years)
Gertrude M. Kildee (4 years)
Stanley J. Alster (2 years)
Julius J. Persensky (2 years)
Mary B. Ward (2 years)

May 1991
Mary B. Ward (4 years)
Julius J. Persensky (4 years)
Stanley J. Alster (4 years)
Sidney A. Katz (2 years)
Gertrude M. Kildee (2 years)

May 1993
Sidney A. Katz (4 years)
Gertrude M. Kildee (4 years)
Stanley J. Alster (2 years)
Julius J. Persensky (2 years)
Mary B. Ward (2 years)

May 1995
Stanley J. Alster (4 years)
Geraldine E. Edens (4 years)
Henry F. Marraffa Jr. (4 years)
Sidney A. Katz (2 years)
Gertrude M. Kildee (2 years)

May 1997
Sidney A. Katz (4 years)
Charles F. Davis (4 years)
Stanley J. Alster (2 years)
Geraldine E. Edens(2 years)
Henry F. Marraffa Jr. (2 years)

This Labor Day parade traveled down Diamond Avenue in the 1950s. (Courtesy of E. Russell Gloyd.)

APPENDIX OF ELECTED OFFICIALS

September 8, 1998
Katz appointed to serve Bohrer's mayoral
term.

November 8, 1998
Bohrer appointed to serve Katz's unexpired
term.

May 1999
Sharon B. Bohrer (4 years)
Stanley J. Alster (4 years)
Geraldine E. Edens (4 years)
Ann T. Somerset (2 years)
Charles F. Davis (2 years)

August 7, 2000
Bohrer resigned, and Marraffa appointed to
serve unexpired term.

November 2001
Stanley J. Alster (4 years)
Geraldine E. Edens (4 years)
Henry F. Marraffa Jr. (4 years)
John B. Schlichting (2 years)
Ann T. Somerset (4 years)

155

BIBLIOGRAPHY

Abert, John J. *Routes for the Proposed Maryland Canal*. 1838.

Anne Arundel Gentry.

Beacht, Ada M. "Gaithersburg Then and Now," "Town Beginnings," "First Capital Improvements," "Election Process," "A Look at the First Charter," "Distress Whistles," and "Forms of Government over 100 Years." Gaithersburg *Gazette*. 1978.

"Establishment of Building Lines." City of Gaithersburg Communique. 1978.

Boyd, T.H.S. *The History of Montgomery County, Maryland from its earliest Settlement in 1650 to 1879*. Clarksburg, MD: 1879.

Christensen, Judy. *Martha Meem's 200 Acres*. City of Gaithersburg, 1996.

Christie, Mollie, et. al. *Script of Centennial Pageant of Gaithersburg*. Gaithersburg Historical Association, 1950.

Cissell, Anne W. *The Montgomery County Story*. 1989.

Dirks, Lee. "The Population Boom and When It Hits." *National Observer*. 7 July 1964.

Farquhar, Roger Brookes. *Old Homes and History of Montgomery County Maryland*. Washington, D.C.: 1952.

Fitzpatrick, John C., ed. *The Diary of George Washington, 1748–1799*.

Hanson, Dr. Royce. *Importance of Agriculture in Montgomery County*. December 1977.

Heart, Elizabeth Witzgall. "Landmarks of Gaithersburg" and "Gaithersburg's Religious Faiths." 1995.

Heart, William Hutchinson. "Gaithersburg and the Railroad."

Hutchinson, William E. Gaithersburg: *The Heart of Montgomery County*. Gaithersburg, MD: 1978.

Lipscomb, Lee. *Gaithersburg, Its Advantages*. Gaithersburg, MD: 1891.

MacMaster, Richard K. and Ray Eldon Hiebert. *A Grateful Remembrance: The Story of Montgomery County, Maryland*. Rockville, MD: Montgomery County Historical Society, 1976.

Manuel, Janet. Gaithersburg: *The Heart of Montgomery County*. Gaithersburg, MD: 1978.

Rural Survey in Maryland, A: A Sociological Survey of Montgomery County, Maryland. Department of Church and Country Life of the Board of Home Missions of the Presbyterian Church, 1912.

Scharf, J. Thomas. *History of Western Maryland*. Philadelphia, PA: 1882.

65 Years of Ministry. St. Martin's Roman Catholic Church.

Waters, George Ellsworth. "Gaithersburg's Blacksmith," "Plymouth Rock on Brookes Avenue," and "Justice In Gaithersburg." *GHA News*, April 2000–July 2001.

Watts, Jill. *God, Harlem U.S.A.: The Father Divine Story*. Berkeley, CA: University of California Press, 1992.

Wilson, Loretta S. *Gaithersburg, The Heart of Montgomery County*. Gaithersburg, MD: City of Gaithersburg, 1978.

Witcraft, John R. *Cornelius Jansen Clopper and His Descendants*. Merchantville, NJ: 1912.

Witzgall, Elizabeth Bingham and Rev. Msgr. E. Meyer. *Gaithersburg: The Heart of Montgomery County*.

Other sources include the Archives of Maryland, tax assessment records of Montgomery County, the Montgomery County plat book, the Maryland Historical Trust Historic Sites Survey, land records of Montgomery County and Frederick County, the Town of Gaithersburg minutes, the City of Gaithersburg receipt book and street files, the minutes of the Forest Oak Cemetery Association, and numerous articles from the Frederick *Post*, Evansville *Daily Courier*, and the Montgomery County *Sentinel*, as well as various interviews conducted by Gail Littlefield.

A stablehand holds two horses at W.O. Dosh's Stables on Brookes Avenue.

Index

This photograph of ice skaters on Summit Hall Pond was taken in the 1950s.